The Baby

&

The Bathwater

Copyright Bob Prester, 2010. All Rights Reserved.

About the Cover

The ancients in all cultures studied the heavens (the night skies) and obviously had a cosmic awareness of our relationship with the stars. Groups of stars were anthropomorphized and stories were told about them that related to the ages, when to plant and when to harvest. At some point the sun was seen as masculine and ruled the day. The moon came to be seen as feminine and ruled the night. In the winter, the sun, the energetic source of life on Earth, seemed to be dying. At the winter Solstice (December 22), the sun reached its furthest point in its perceived retreat to the South. It was said that the sun had died. Then for three days, including the 22nd, the sun rose at the same spot on the horizon.

The three stars in Orion's Belt were called the three Kings or three Wise Men. It was said they followed the brightest star in the East (Sirius), and pointed to the exact spot on the horizon where the sun, the light of the world, would rise on the 25th, one degree further North. It was said the sun was born again on that day.

There's a lady who's sure all that glitters is gold and she speaks in symbols and parables about buying humanity's DNA. She stands in the harbor in New York waving the Olympic Torch for those who have eyes but can't see and ears but can't hear. For those who have skin, but can't feel, her name is Columbia and she drives a car whose license plate reads "Taxation without representation." For those who have noses, but can't smell, and tongues, but can't taste, she sells coffee at Starbucks so that those who are soundly sleeping on the Corporate Altar can pretend to be wide awake.

She's been pregnant for over 200 years and just recently gave birth in time for the programmed apocalypse written about in Revelation. As Marlon Brando said in Francis Ford Coppola's movie about this "Apocalypse Now" programming, "The Horror!" That's the idea.

There's a contract she's trying to terrorize the baby into signing – "Order Out of Chaos". The small print says, "I, spiritually aware Humanity, give up, of my own free will, my freedom, for the security of a microchip and a global New World Order."

This book is written on the Baby's behalf and dedicated in the names of my Wife, Sylvia, Myself, and our Son, David, to the Spiritual awakening of Humanity currently underway.

Bon Voyage –

Bob

Cover Art by Dave Shure

"Courage is contagious. When a brave man takes a stand, the spines of others are stiffened." - Billy Graham

from page 226 of "The Day You Were Born" by Linda Joyce

The Baby & The Bathwater

Chapter One

It's All About the O

(The Divine Order of Everything)

Out In Empty Sky

If you catch a fragrance of the unseen, Like that, you will not be able

To be contained. You will be out in empty sky.

Any beauty the world has, any desire, will easily be yours.

As you live deeper in the heart, the mirror gets clearer and cleaner.

Shams of Tabriz realized God in himself. When that happens, you have no anxieties about losing anyone or anything. You break the spells that human difficulties cause.

Interpretations come, hundreds, from all the religious symbols and parables and prayers.

You know what they mean, when the Presence lives through you.

October 24, - A Year With Rumi - Coleman Barks

What You Are

What I Am

Being Human – Human Being

There is an Awareness, so basic, so fundamental to humanity that to be without it, or leave it unacknowledged, or to twist it into a tool for subjugating others, is, to those who are aware of it, subhuman. This Awareness is spirituality, the Truth Vibration. In the Human species we refer to it as the awareness of being aware, our being-ness. There's a spiritual awakening taking place on this planet right now that will fundamentally change the experience of life here forever.

This ain't it.   ~~$4.49~~ $4.17

We're all experiencing the awakening in our own, personal, unique, way. I'm writing this book because I became conscious of this awakening. I realize that it can seem very scary to everyone who hasn't made the conscious connection with what and who they truly are. Many of us consciously symbolize the infinite and the eternal with the name "God", and visualize God as a Grand Male Deity with a long white beard.

We've been programmed through Religions and Education to perceive the infinite and eternal in this manner and to subjugate ourselves to it as being far less than, and separate from it. This is a subtle type of Trojan Horse, which has been inserted into our collective consciousness and has virtually turned Humanity into an energetic resource for a ruthless cabal of spiritual depravity.

From the inside out.

The Current spiritual awakening is associated with the true nature of Creation and authentic time. Nothing ever happened in the past and nothing will ever happen in the future. It all happens now. Everything happens in the infinite and eternal Present and is not spiritually dependent on a Grand Old Man with a long white beard.

Ho, Ho, Ho………

No, really, we have been, and are being, deceived on a massive scale, from the inside out and it all happened, is happening, and will happen only, in the infinite and eternal Now. Our left-brain, through which we interact physically, in this dimension, has been programmed to create an ego or individualized personality. Through this, ultimately bogus image of our self we've learned to see ourselves as male or female, black or white, tall or short, fat or skinny, fast or slow, straight or gay, pretty or ugly, weak or strong, smart or dumb, etc. Through this same image we see ourselves in a linear fashion through time, as variously, young, teenage, adult, middle age, and old-timer. This all has to do with our identification of ourselves with the physical. There's nothing evil about recognizing our physicality, but when it's heavily weighted in importance when compared with the right-brained awareness, our spiritual nature, unity consciousness, the infinite and eternal, it leaves us wide open for manipulation and corruption. As this spiritual awakening continues, everyone, religious or not, will ultimately attract that awareness into their consciousness. For those who've dedicated their lives to religious pursuits, this might at first feel like the "Incomprehensible Demoralization" Bill Wilson talks about in his literature on alcoholism. That's because religions are simply another addiction that has been used by those with Occult awareness, to subvert our natural spiritual awareness for their own purposes. Those purposes are rather simple and fear-based. By getting us to perceive things from a perspective of lack, fear, and separation, we can be convinced of our own free will to subjugate ourselves to the unknown and give it credit for our own innate Being-ness. Perceiving ourselves as separate from the Divine, we can easily be divided and manipulated against each other out of fear for the advantage of those who gave us our religions, our politics, and our monetary system.

"The music is speeding up and there's not enough to go around."

It comes wrapped in all the trappings of authentic spiritual awareness such as Love, Tolerance, Forgiveness, Patience, Humility, Faith, etc.

But because we now see ourselves as separate, and unworthy, we can be indoctrinated with dogma such as the need for a savior. We can be taught to hold two diametrically opposed beliefs in the name of God, such as "Thou shalt not kill," and "Thou shalt wipe them out thoroughly off the face of the Earth." No one is allowed to question the Authority who instructs us who to kill because the orders came from God. We are required to identify ourselves with our egos and subjugate ourselves to an external Deity who pretends to grant us access to our right-brained awareness when we die. If you're one of those who have attracted the awareness of duality into your consciousness and suddenly find yourself adrift with the God of your misunderstanding exposed as an incarnation of the Wizard of Oz, this book is for you. Our programmed tendency at this point is to "Throw the baby out with the bath water."

Not a Good Idea

David Icke says, "The Universe wraps up its greatest gifts and hands them to us as our worst nightmares." This is the awareness behind the spiritual axiom, "Pain is the touchstone of all spiritual growth." When this happens to conditioned and indoctrinated people, often they become suicidal or contemplate walking on the "dark side" with disastrous consequences. We've been programmed, not least, through our language (Neuro Linguistic Programming), to think like that. When I became consciously aware that the Christian Religion was a ruse, I decided to join the Marine Corps which violated many of the principles I used to hold as true, simply because my faith had been shattered and the Marine Corps seemed to be a legitimate way for me to redeem my self esteem at the time (1984). These radical swings between light and dark are exactly how mankind, as a species, has been conditioned to create up until now. I was already an alcoholic and a drug addict with no conscious intention to wake up spiritually. Unconsciously, I'd attracted into my life the ability to move outside of my previous comfort zone. I didn't consciously think I wanted to give my authentic spiritual energy in this dimension to become a killing machine for the Occult power behind Corporate America. I thought, as I'd been programmed to think, that I was just growing up and was now willing to do my patriotic duty and serve my country, defending Life, Liberty, and the pursuit of Happiness, from the forces of evil. Synchronistically, 1984, the book by the same name, and unwittingly becoming government property by signing the contract to join the Marine Corps, have so much in common. Most recruits don't realize that in joining the military they're voluntarily giving up the rights as a citizen that they believe they're fighting for. Being slightly jaded myself, I took the "so what else is new" approach and focused on the drinking man's paradise I'd now found myself a part of. It didn't take long for me to accidentally run afoul of the Big Green Marine Machine. As a result, the Marine Corps put me through their intense rehab, which made me aware, over time, that I was an alcoholic and a drug addict. This knowledge was not enough to keep me clean and sober in the Marine Corps. Through the synchronicity of a second lieutenant, five years my junior, who I'd grown up with at a Lutheran boarding school in southeastern Madagascar, I was discharged from the Marine Corps. I began to take a serious look at my drug and alcohol addiction.

Neuro-Cardio Linguistics

Alcoholics Anonymous speaks the language of the heart.

Alcoholics Anonymous speaks the language of the heart. Consequently there's a massive public misperception of it. If we speak the language of the heart in public, we soon find ourselves ostracized, ridiculed or compartmentalized as light-headed because in public, the intellect and the dollar are worshipped over the heart which is perceived as weak and effeminate, subconsciously. Basically Alcoholics Anonymous is perceived as group therapy for individuals who deal with their problems by drinking too much.

Those who do not recognize the language of the heart, both in and out of twelve step fellowships, are at a loss to come up with an accurate understanding of the difference between Religion's approach to spiritual illness, Psychiatry's approach, and the Twelve Steps…except perhaps to note that the language is a little saltier in A.A.

Society recognized the phenomenal impact A.A. was having on alcohol addiction and assimilated it into "the system." So if you find yourself charged with an alcohol-related offense in the United States, you'll likely find yourself auditing A.A. by law, for a period of time. Paradoxically, it's not a fellowship for those who need it, or want it, but only for those who actually *use* it, and that is an inside job. ***Understanding the primary importance of teaching and comprehending our spiritual nature and the Unity Consciousness it involves is a most important message.*** When this understanding is a primary concern, it becomes easy to perceive the intentions behind an economic, profit-motivated, monetary system, based on debt that thrives on scarcity. When this understanding is a primary awareness, it's easy to perceive the intentions behind philosophies based on fear, sexual domination, elitism, hierarchy, and legalism. The primary importance of the spiritual nature of everything is a message of Unity and Oneness. It's the authentic foundation upon which we can build an authentic world of integrity and Love. It is the awareness from which our societies and cultures came and have been subverted intentionally, by deception and sorcery, through fear, by a few who use their Occult knowledge to divide and conquer, using our ignorance of who and what we are to maintain power and control in this dimension. By teaching lies in the name of truth, and coloring the truth to look weak, impotent, or even evil, we've been manipulated into giving our authentic spiritual power to the lie which is then used to finance tyranny in another part of the world, which we perceive as separate from us by virtue of race, religion, or nationality…usually all three. Our spiritual nature is the most important concept to grasp in this dimension. ***Breaking through this manipulated division is the reason for alcoholism and addictions in general. We became addicts as a means to sedate and control the natural emotions created by false constructs of division through which we allow ourselves to perceive "war" as a "necessary evil."*** -What Crap!

USMC Major General Smedley D. Butler

USMC Major General Smedley D. Butler

War is a racket and we're being manipulated through fear to perceive it as just the nature of the real world. Unbelievable Crap! Here are the first few lines from two-time Congressional Medal of Honor winner, Major General Smedley D. Butler's book:

War is a racket. It always has been.

It is possibly the oldest, easily the most profitable, surely the most vicious. It is the only one international in scope. It is the only one in which the profits are reckoned in dollars and the losses in lives.

A racket is best described, I believe, as something that is not what it seems to the majority of the people. Only a small "inside" group knows what it is about. It is conducted for the benefit of the very few, at the expense of the very many. Out of war a few people make huge fortunes.

In the World War [I] a mere handful garnered the profits of the conflict. At least 21,000 new millionaires and billionaires were made in the United States during the World War. That many admitted their huge blood gains in their income tax returns. How many other war millionaires falsified their tax returns no one knows.

[Top Contractors 2007](#)

Lockheed Martin Corp	$27,320,616,068
Boeing Company	$20,861,418,121
Northrop Grumman Corp	$16,769,641,720
General Dynamics Corp	$11,472,032,564
Raytheon Company	$10,411,293,335

KBR Inc.	$ 5,972,078,973
L-3 Communications	$ 5,039,851,150
United Technologies Corp	$ 4,574,841,469
BAE Systems	$ 4,500,683,821
SAIC	$ 3,404,387,189
General Electric Company	$ 2,933,412,009

The only reason we continue to buy the concept of war as a legitimate enterprise is because of our ignorance of our true spiritual nature. We are everything that exists. We are each other. Not a piece of the whole, the whole enchilada … experiencing life subjectively. Along the way we got frightened. This manifested in our selling our authentic spirituality as a concept of primary importance. It's a lie based on fear. Because of this manipulation, we've developed addictions to religions, political ideologies, sex, money, food, drugs, weapons and technology. Evil contains within it the seeds of its own destruction. These addictions and the system's programmed insustainability will, over time, attract incredible pain into our lives. When the pain of the addiction becomes greater than the pain we're using the addiction to medicate, we begin to realize, as Einstein said, "you can't solve a problem with the same level of consciousness that created it." This is spiritual awakening. As more and more people wake up to **Who** and **What** they are, the world that we're creating because of who and what *we* are changes radically. ***We're on the brink of a quantum leap in this dimension because of that.*** The only thing holding us back is the integration of the awareness of who and what we truly are. At this point in what we think of as time, we're waking up to the fact that those we allow to manipulate us do not have our best interests at heart.

At the same time we're realizing that these perverts only have the power that they do because we're giving it to them. Bombs, Torture, Nuclear, Chemical, and Biological weapons of mass destruction, lethal injection, hanging, and electrocution will be things of the non-spiritually aware past. We will no longer study and glorify war because we know who and what we are. Reverence for life will be taught and felt from conception without the need for laws and bureaucracies. The suppression of **Who** and **What** we are is behind all the fear, greed, and hate.

Prayer & Meditation

Shall we start with a little prayer? Our Rupert Murdoch who art one of many Occult personages we've unwittingly been worshipping with our money. Blind Spot is thy name; Zion.

Thy kingdom come.

Thy will be done, on Earth, as it is in the Corporate Boardroom. Give us this day our daily programming and forgive us our lapses in Groupthink as we try our best to make everyone else conform. Lead us not into hot water with Our Bosses, but deliver us from scumbag non-conformists. For thine is the kingdom and the power and the glory forever and ever. Ahhhhh-men.

I started out writing this book knowing that, for me, nothing else was more important. I'd become aware at a very deep, personal level, once again, that things were not as they seemed. I realized that there were many who had figured this out and there were some who were using their awareness of it to control the greater part of humanity. This is done through controlling our thoughts. Controlling people's thoughts is not as difficult as it might seem. If people are not aware of who and what they are – they can be subtly influenced, over time, into believing they're something they're not. Because of this, humanity has become a resource for something else that is not what it seems. This something else is not human, and it is most definitely, *not* God. This subject, by its very nature, is infinitely complicated and confusing *if* things aren't kept in their proper order. Since I'm talking about what "is" and "is not" God here, I'll refer to it as "the Divine order of things." Like which came first, the chicken or the egg? Groupthink would have us believe that is just a meaningless riddle. This book is specifically about how important that riddle is and the dire implications for those in this world who keep getting the answer wrong. It is helpful to understand that the egg is symbolic of the spiritual and the chicken is symbolic of the physical.

Humpty Dumpty

(First Things First – The Egg before the Chicken)

Carefully and thoughtfully, putting pen to paper and writing, - Don't put the cart before the horse – I thought, "that's it!" But what did it mean? Could it have anything to do with, "Which came first, the chicken or the egg?" Did it have anything to do with "Ladies first"? Who was this Humpty Dumpty character and why did society consider him/her such an important character to learn about so early on, in life? I would plant my tongue firmly in my cheek and use the scientific approach.

Humpty Dumpty was an egg, of course. The egg is symbolic of the Divine Feminine, the spiritual, the infinite and eternal. Like the professional who's trying to sell you some overstocked merchandise on TV says, "It's all about the 'O'." O is a symbol of the spiritual universe, everything that exists. Of course the Pro that's saying, "It's all about the 'O'," doesn't explain that crucial bit. Humpty Dumpty sat on a wall. Scientifically we understand that this is simply a metaphor for her divine ambivalence. She could go one way or the other or she could stay on top of the wall between the left and the right, where she belongs, like the Pineal gland. This is a woman's prerogative. Scientifically, we can discern that this must have been what Jesus was referring to when he said, "Blasphemy against the Holy Spirit will never be forgiven." Jesus, who must have been a parable himself, wasn't giving us the keys to the nuclear powered DeLorean and daring us to blow it up. He was saying, "Ladies first, get it wrong and it won't work." "Understand that you are the divine, infinite, and eternal, spirit, first, last, and always. Forget that crucial piece of information, forget that **you** are *in* the world, but not *of* the world, and you'll be stuck on a prison planet of incompetent monarchs until you work it out." Humpty Dumpty had a great fall. Somebody obviously got it wrong. That somebody must have been the monarchy. All the king's horses and all the king's men couldn't put Humpty together again? That king couldn't have been very bright in the first place, using his horses to put an egg back together. Then, the fact that we are taught this ultimate bit of wisdom in kindergarten allows the king to say he told us the truth and we chose to believe that Jesus was giving a 5 year old the keys to the nuclear DeLorean. It was so tragic what happened; forever and ever.

So, you see, using the scientific method, several tongues and a little cheek, we've completely unraveled the mystery of Humpty Dumpty and which came first, the chicken or the egg. It does not imply that one gender is superior to the other or that right is better than left, or dark is better than light. It's all about the "O". God is One; right *and* left, dark *and* light, female *and* male. Separate them first and make one better than the other and you're stuck with all the *king's* horses *and* all the *king's men* trying to put Humpty together again and of course you're going to need a judge to pass judgment that cannot be questioned. In other words, get the order wrong and kiss the truth goodbye. Don't put the cart before the horse...ever. We are spiritual first, last, and always. We're physical manifestations of the infinite and eternal "O"ne, *only* because we're spiritually everything that exists, *first.* Lose that awareness and Bill Gate's and David Rockefeller's finest teams of horses will work their whole lifetimes trying to put your egg back together, charging you a seemingly very economical fee for their efforts, to no avail, but the funeral will be dazzling. Necrophilia…it's all about the "O". That's why it's so important to learn Humpty Dumpty in kindergarten. Unfortunately, all the king's horses and all the king's men neglected to interpret it for you, so competitive sports and war as a means of determining truth began to make some kind of insane sense. This is also why speaking in tongues, to kindergartners, without an interpreter is not just silly, it's dangerous. We're all learning to follow the truth where it leads. We're learning the truth discerner is within us, the individual, on an individual basis. Be true to yourself. The truth is within you. Some of you might be able to perceive that THAT is what I'm doing here and now, being true to myself. Oh, and by the way, "Professional" is just a happy name for prostitute. Really. I should know. Don't follow leaders. Follow your heart.

-From Eckhart Tolle's 2009 Calendar – December –

True salvation is fulfillment, peace, life in all its fullness. It is to be who you are, to feel within you the good that has no opposite, the joy of being that depends on nothing outside itself. True salvation is to know yourself as an inseparable part of the timeless and formless One life from which all that exists derives its being.

Paradox

As we become more spiritually aware, we perceive paradox more often. Paradox is about perspective…in time. My father and I can be looking at the same thing from different perspectives in time and perceive it in the moment as its opposite. Paul Simon wrote a song about apartment life called "One man's ceiling is another man's floor" that reveals this paradigm. Unless we keep the divine order of things as a priority, it's very logical that we're going to put the cart before the horse. Unless we're taught, and we in turn teach, the Sacred Priority of "First things First", we're going to become subjects of hierarchy and tyranny. It's all about the O.

The ancient Eastern "Yin Yang" symbolizes the paradox of the divine feminine (dark) and the divine masculine (light) as a complete, balanced, whole. Using the language of science, Newton described this principle as an underlying law of motion. For every action, there's an equal and opposite reaction.

The indigo point within the circle or target sign, symbolizes the union of the divine masculine within the divine feminine, the physical manifesting from the spiritual; an authentic metaphor.

The circle represents the serenity to accept the things we cannot change, the Holy Spirit, or the Divine Feminine. The point within the circle represents the courage to change the things we can, or the divine masculine; the creative force. "First things first" is the wisdom to know the difference. The infinite and eternal *is* what makes the finite and temporal possible. Everyone, male and female is born of a Woman. This isn't talking about the "Goddess" or the divine right of Queens to rule. It's talking about our own personal psychic sovereignty. Cognizance of the spiritual is a must before there can be authentic progress in the physical. The egg always precedes the chicken. Don't put the cart before the horse. If we do we'll find ourselves in court, seriously arguing our case before a judge whose decisions cannot be questioned and the question will be, "which came first the chicken or the egg?" If you don't already know the answer, you'll see yourself as a victim and gamble everything on the judge deciding in your favor. Spirituality is an inside job. It's about awareness of your own inner psychic sovereignty, your profound responsibility to be true to yourself and in so doing, being true to everyone else. My Father perceived the Christian Religion as the truth. Paradoxically, I perceived it as a parable that had been manipulated into being taken literally. As I see my reflection in my Father and he sees his reflection in me, we transcend religion and politics and discern the

Sacred. Infinite and eternal Love is the only Truth. To me, authentically communicating the truth as discerned by the heart is integral to Humanity's survival as co-creators in this dimension. The ancient esoteric stories about the Christ, used to pass on the connection between the Heavens (spiritual) & the Earth (Physical) through being true to your heart (the Christ) have been hijacked by something that is not connected spiritually. We have the capacity to believe that an infinite and eternal hierarchy of fear (Religion) is the only truth. We've been testing that theory out in time. Time is the bathwater.

Chapter Two

Who Are You?

God Bless The Child

Billie Holiday/ Arthur Herzog Jr.

Them that's got shall get
Them that's not shall lose
So the Bible said and it still is news
Mama may have, Papa may have
But God bless the Child that's got his own
That's got his own

Yes, the strong gets more
While the weak ones fade
Empty pockets don't ever make the grade
Mama may have, Papa may have
But God bless the child that's got his own
That's got his own

Money, you've got lots of friends
Crowding round the door
When you're gone, spending ends
They don't come no more
Rich relations give
Crust of bread and such
You can help yourself
But don't take too much
Mama may have, Papa may have
But God bless the child that's got his own
That's got his own

Mama may have, Papa may have
But God bless the child that's got his own
That's got his own
He just worry about nothin'
Cause he's got his own

Who I Am

Revealing The Concealed

10 – 13 – 1955

Please allow me to introduce myself...

The Great Commission

I was contacted in the Gregorian Calendar year of 2008 and told to write this book – primarily to God's chosen people, the Alcoholics, but eventually to the Greeks, and then ultimately; everybody. Apparently God wanted to clear up a few common misconceptions that seem to have stirred up some confusion about the nature of God as perceived by 6 & ¾ billion poor people for the benefit of a relative few extremely wealthy Satanic Sorcerers and

interbreeding sadistic hypnotists. Really.

God is a Duck. This is the awareness from which we get the phrase, "You could have knocked me over with a feather." It refers to the state of shock the "average mortal" finds themselves in when the old man who prefers to be talked to in Victorian English is revealed as a charlatan or "a quack", and they find themselves confronting the reality of their own inner Duck. I know, I know, it flies in the face of conventional wisdom sort of like "conventional produce", which is probably why it took so long for it to come out.

It's not that God's been trying to keep it a secret or anything. She asked Donald Trump to tell the world, but Donald, being esoterically hip, and knowing how to keep a secret while advertising, named himself after his favorite duck and went around pretending he was God. No, it's my job and one I've shouldered proudly even though predominantly unconsciously, since October 13, 1955.

This is the real meaning behind the phrase, "If it walks like a duck and quacks like a duck...it's probably a duck."

This was God's way of telling the world that Alcoholics are her chosen people. She thought that by only saving Noah the first go around, people would have figured that out, but no, people are still trying to figure out what, in the flock, she's talking about. She's basically saying, "If you've got one foot in the past (yesterday), and one foot in the future (tomorrow)......you're going to be a piece of cake to manipulate."

Plaque at the entrance of Disneyland that embodies the intended spirit by Walt Disney: to leave reality and enter fantasy.

The Esoterically Hip Uncle Waltzy & Friends

The early Native Americans were well aware of this and left glyphs on the rocks of stickmen with a duck for a head to indicate they knew the deal long before the Great White Father brought them firewater, smallpox, and casinos. Contrary to what you may have been reading, this Native American glyph art creator was not an earlier incarnation of Donald Trump, but of Joseph Smith, who, while perhaps not being a very "good" artist, was definitely a Freemason. The Latter Day Saint, Eddie Izzard, who is not a Mormon, but is a Saint none the less, almost let the cat out of the bag during his early comedy routines. Commenting on God's decision to kill every living thing on the face of the Earth except for Noah, his family and the one righteous couple of every living species on the planet, he pointed out that 40 days and 40 nights of rain are probably not going to make a really big dent in the bad duck population. The concept of God being a duck flew right over his head. Bad fish by the boatload must have survived too. Then you realize that the bad ducks had to have something to eat. The ancient bunny populations were particularly heinous in that they were born and raised with their clothes on and never really took them off – yet they managed to procreate like minks. The heart of an alcoholic cannot comprehend that level of depravity. This is the most likely reason Noah got drunk after surviving the original Katrina and took his clothes off. He was probably reduced to eating quite a few bunnies after the deluge. I saw Elton John, who must be one of Gods chosen people, dressed up like a duck one night, or maybe it was a peacock, and for a second I thought he was going to start quacking. But he just sang, "Goodbye yellow brick road" and "Don't let the sun go down on me" and I knew he was going to leave the job up to me.

It's ok. I'm a man. I can take it. I guess this is the time to let you all know that I'm one of God's chosen people too. Yeah of course it was a shock, you could have knocked me over with a feather when it first hit me. I'm not going to dress up like a duck. You have to draw the line somewhere. If you don't stand for something, you'll fall for anything, especially if you have to make $100,000.00 annually just to keep up with the Joneses and have a warm place to see a man about a dog. By now you've probably guessed that the Baby and the Bath Water is a euphemism for something. You're right! The Baby is us; God's chosen people. The Bath Water is everything else; Hurricane Katrina. It's ok. It's just a bath. For some it's a Baptism for others it's a birth. For the Rothschilds, Rockefellers, Windsors and other Zionist Establishment Fat Cats it's Bye-Bye. All of us are going to be discovering in our own special way that those we gave our power to, in places of authority and trust, have abused that power particularly badly, or shall I say, on purpose, and lied to us about it for their own personal gain. We as a species are going to become crystal clear as to the importance of being true to ourselves. We'll no longer be able to pretend that we think "collateral damage" was ever ok. We'll no longer be able to pretend that torture is ever an option for sane people. We don't need laws to tell us these things. We're going to learn that we're all ducks and we're all God's chosen people, and that just as we're capable of unbelievable stupidity and arrogance motivated by fear, we're capable of incredible grace and power motivated by truth. "Infinite Love is the only truth, everything else is illusion." – David Icke. We're going to learn to forgive ourselves and others, admit when we're wrong and hold fast when we're right, and then we're going to learn the meaning of conscious co-creation. First we've got to understand that we're the ones responsible for what we believe, nobody else. This is the meaning behind the phrase "Fool me once, shame on you. Fool me twice, shame on me." Or "Once bitten, twice shy." The reality for us as God's chosen people has been more like, "Fool me once, thank you sir, may I have another?" until we finally reached the place where we realized that our conscious connection with our own inner Duck had been severely compromised. It was at this juncture that it began to become clear to us that without the Duck of our understanding, we were slaves to a vicious tyrant. At first we had to look outside of ourselves for the reflection of the Duck of our understanding. In other words, when it became obvious to us that our God, "Money" was a false God, we had to learn to love our neighbors as ourselves all over again. By doing that we began to heal our conscious connection with our own inner Duck and paraDucksically, with the one true Duck, through whom we all live and breathe and have our being. It's not Santa Claus! This phrase is going to become especially poigniant in the next few years……er, make that millenia – "Love will get you through times of no money better than money will get you through times of no love."

Revealing The Concealed

Back in the early 60's, Bob Dylan hitch-hiked his way to New York City to find his inspiration, Woody Guthrie. He found himself in the middle of the Bohemian, socially awakening, artistically creative, beatnik scene, happening in clubs like "The Gaslight." There he met Dave Van Ronk who had stylized his own version of "The House Of The Rising Sun". Dylan recognized the depth of the song and played it on one of his earliest recordings. It made the song famous until Eric Burdon and the Animals recorded it and took it to another level in pop culture. Most everyone who heard the song could feel a deep connection to it, but couldn't quite consciously put together why it was such an important song. *That's my job* – Revealing the concealed.

In the early 90's, when I was about 7 years clean and sober (I got sober in "86), I was facing some huge emotional hurdles having to do with finances, belief, and responsibility. I was being pulled in many different directions, each one claiming some sort of holy priority to my time and energy. I made a decision to focus on my spiritual path through Alcoholics Anonymous and let go of the rest. I was sponsoring a guy at the time who set me up with my first computer and a user friendly, (among other things) internet provider. This opened the door for me to a world of information that I had suspected and had been looking for from people and sources that unconsciously blocked that information because of conditioning.

I had a very conscious close encounter as a child in Congo with an entity that was non-human. Suddenly I was finding voluminous quantities of highly credible affirmation on the subject, where up until then; there had been none, with exceptions like George Lukas and Steven Speilberg, who seemed to be dealing in fantasy although I knew there was more to it. In all the areas I was interested in studying such as Extra Terrestrials/ UFO's, alternative energy sources, alternative medicine, spirituality, quantum physics...one man's name kept surfacing; David Icke. David Icke has become known as the world's foremost Conspiracy Researcher and Exposer. To me, that's like saying the Pope is the world's most pre-eminent cross-dresser. It's accurate from a certain perspective, but you're really missing the bulk of what's going on, especially in light of how the "mainstream" treats the subject of Conspiracy.

David Icke made me aware in clear, precise, easily verifiable terms, how an "elite" bloodline predating recorded history, had been manipulating the entire human species through suppressed "Occult" knowledge, multi-dimensional awareness, religion, finances, education, sex, fear, and medicine or drugs, but that's just a taste of what David Icke is doing. Much of this "Occult" knowledge comes from what we call the Kabbalah. This ancient knowledge encompasses Astrotheology, Astrology, Numerology, the Tarot, and much of what we in the West have been conditioned and indoctrinated to call "Pagan", "Sorcery", and "Witchcraft." I was intrigued about the Kabbalah and sent off for some literature and tapes on the subject. One of the books was "The 72 Names of God", a meditation book from Rabbi, Yehuda Berg. Along with the book, if you give them your birthday, they will tell you your name, among the 72 names of God, according to ancient Kabbalistic astrology. On becoming aware of my name, according to the Kabbalah, I realized they had put me back in touch with my birth vision within this physical matrix. I was born on the Anniversary of the day that the Roman Catholic Church excommunicated, with a vengeance, the Knights Templar, with their red crosses, their gold, and their arches. This is the day we memorialize as Friday the 13th without knowing why. This happened on October 13, 1307 or about 703 years ago. My name in the Kabbalah's 72 Names of God is: Mem Yud Kaf, in Hebrew, which means, "Revealing the Concealed" in English. In his books, David Icke reveals that the Knights Templar had discovered the true source and nature of the Church's power and were blackmailing the church, using their newfound Occult knowledge to build Cathedrals on specific locations all over Europe. The Pope and the Kings of the era (especially Philip the Fair of France) found this very threatening to their power and collaborated to rid themselves of the Knights Templar in secrecy on Friday, October 13, 1307, using the Kabbalistic day for "Revealing the Concealed." The surviving Templars fled to Scotland and founded what we now know as Freemasonry & Piracy. Eventually they made their way to America and founded what we now know as The United States of America & the CIA. We live in a world of illusion that we create through ignorance for the benefit of sorcerers. That's changing now, thank God.

Chris Carter who produced and directed "The X Files" was born on the same day I was, a year later, and because of his Kabbalistic awareness, he advertises that fact all through the series. The X Files is all about "Revealing the Concealed" in a manner that promotes " The Truth Is Out There" without most of the viewing audience having a clue. The pilot episode of "The Lone Gunman", a spin-off of the X files, was about a ruthless cabal, flying a plane into the World Trade Center. He was exposing what was planned to happen on September 11, 2001 without actually exposing it. Only those who are sworn to secrecy understand what is brazenly going on. Because of the level of conditioning and indoctrination (mind control), those who are actually seeing through this façade are painted as "conspiracy nuts" by their own "friends" and "families". This episode aired on National television before September 11, 2001 and even longer before George W. Bush and Condoleeza Rice claimed on the record, with a straight face, that **no one** anticipated **just that**. The video "Zeitgeist" records their bald face lies as "Commander-in-Chief" & "Secretary of State" of the Nation. 9/11 is a numerological way of saying "Without God" or "Skipping God." Ten, numerologically speaking, is the union of the divine masculine, 1, with the divine feminine, 0. The Zionist Media Magnate Rupert Murdoch's FOX network has a numerological meaning too. Freeman of the "Freeman Perspective" breaks it down for us on his web site of the same name:

666 The Number Of The Beast

If we calculate the number of the beast we find many interesting connections to the corporate world. Consider that if you transliterate the numbers 666 into English you get FOX. This is how it works: F is the 6th letter of the alphabet, O is the 15th, and X is the 24th, the final computation is 6, 1+5=6, and 2+4=6. So, we have 20th Century Fox, Fox Searchlight (referring to Lucifer) and Fox Mulder. It has been shown that Fox and Scully's characters can be equated with the story of Osiris and Isis. Looking into the numerology in the X-Files we find the Chris Carters Production Company is ten-thirteen. This is the infamous Friday the 13th when the Templars were burnt at the stake. Chris Carter showed us the entire "Truth" about 9/11 in the pilot episode of

"The Lone Gunmen", a spin-off from the X-Files and this psi-op show is used to discredit anything "out of the ordinary".

Lets go a little deeper. The type of magic that is being practiced by our leaders is Kabala. This is based in Hebrew. Therefore, in Hebrew 666 would look like VVV because 6=V in Hebrew. The VW logo incorporates the VVV in its logo with 2 V's interlaced making a third, equaling 666. The 2 V's symbolize the number of the Qlippoth; of the "Dark Side". See our president "VV" as he stands in front of the Woodrow Wilson Center For Science with the interlaced VV's. That's a lot of Beasts!

So by being true to myself and following my heart, I gained some insight into my birth vision once again. You too have a birth vision, which, if you realize the importance of being true to yourself, making it a priority, and learn to listen to and follow your heart, you'll glimpse once again and be able to bring into focus. The times we're living in are very conducive to this kind of work. My birth vision is about revealing that the truth is within us and the importance of simply following the truth where it leads.

The
House of The Rising Son

Chapter Three

A House Divided On Purpose

General Electric is a monolithic Corporation and a huge defense contractor.

G. E. owns N. B. C. and makes incredible profits off of war.

It would not be an exaggeration to say that war is good for G.E. The American People have a collective awareness of the quote attributed to Jesus, "A house divided against itself cannot stand." Another quote attributed to Jesus that seems to be quite familiar to the general populous is: "You cannot serve God and Mammon." These are generally accepted as authentically true, common sense, and valid, no matter what your religion or cultural heritage. To me it's patently obvious that a nation who holds those spiritual concepts to be true on the one hand and allows a huge defense contractor to control a major source of information on the other, is a nation heading for collapse, unless the insanity is recognized and corrected. More than that, it's obvious that any government that would allow such a blatant conflict of interest to exist and go unchecked and unacknowledged, would by the nature of the responsibilities of their jobs, have to be complicit in the conspiriacy to defraud the American

People at the most basic levels. The outrageousness of this offense is compounded everywhere you look. The idea that our former Vice President and former Secretary of Defense under the administrations of our former President and his Father, Dick Cheney, was C.E.O. of Halliburton in between administrations is morally and ethically repugnant to a degree that's hard to verbally express politely, in mixed company. Halliburton is the corporation that comes to mind when people mention the Military Industrial Complex. Even those who did not grow up under the cloud of Fascism, the ideology of Corporatism, should easily recognize the conflict generated when Peace-loving people give their power and decision-making over to a man who gets rich off of war.

We are not our brains, (thank God!) and we are not our bodies although they're both infinitely useful to us in this dimension. **God knows it's "time" we started paying attention to what we believe, because through our beliefs we're creating a nightmare.** Over and over again, I keep being guided to the awareness of how we've been manipulated into seeing ourselves as spiritually broken and separate from the infinite One. I'll describe what I mean.

Christianity, Judaism, and Islam are three separate and distinct Religions that have at their core a belief in an Omnipotent (all powerful), Omniscient, (all knowing), and Omnipresent, (existing everywhere and every when – infinite and eternal) "Father" God. The overt reference to this Supreme Deity being male is clear and unmistakable in all three Religions. Without getting lost in the weeds, let's focus on the Omnipresence of this "Father" God. This means, without reservations, that the Divine Masculine exists in its infinite and eternal completeness within everything that exists. I have no problem accepting that. By focusing on this simple concept from time to time over a lifetime, it's become blatantly clear to me that by omitting conscious validation of the Divine Feminine in our reference to the spiritual source of all, we've allowed ourselves to be subtly deceived into dividing our spiritual house and show favoritism to one side, voluntarily. By subtly adding one sex to the equation for the Dominion, the Power, and the Glory, forever, the dice have been loaded in favor of "the House" and "the House" will always win, when people play with those dice.

Speaking In Tongues

Using "The House" as a metaphor, I'd like to point out my interpretation of "The House Of The Rising Sun" and see if you notice any hints of a metaphor going on yourself. Secret Societies such as the Freemasons are unquestionably used by the powers that be, controlling world events today, and like the Egyptians and the Babylonians before them, use the "Rising Sun" as a metaphor for their ability to manipulate the world. Horus was the ancient Egyptian "Sun" and "Son" of "God." Horus is the root word from which we derive our current words, "hours" and "horizon." Does anybody really know what time it is? I think these guys do. Verizon, the cell phone company whose towers have replaced banks, whose buildings replaced churches, as the tallest structures in town, derives its name from the combination of the Latin words for "True" and "Horizon." You don't have to look far in corporate or political symbolism to see this metaphor played out all over the world today, just as in

ancient times.

Banks, Phone Companies, Oil Companies, Newspapers, Hotel Chains, States, Countries, etc. all use the sun to symbolize what they represent. Set was the Egyptian name for the God of the underworld, or devil, hence the term "sunset." This all seems harmless enough until you take the time to understand what is really being communicated by what we are unconsciously condoning in this consensus trance we find we've been living. Just as polarizing and weighting one side or sex of the God of our understanding has subtle, immediate and infinite effects on how we perceive reality in the moment – so does symbolism of all descriptions. **Ian Xel Lundgold** did an incredible job of exposing how Pope Gregory accomplished focusing Human consciousness on the "**physical world only**" by way of the calendar in his presentation called The "Mayan Calendar Comes North." As of this writing, it can still be found on Youtube. He was one of many bright lights whose lives were tragically cut short while exposing this hidden knowledge.

Once the connection with the inauthentic use of symbolism is made, it's fairly straightforward to trace the symbolism back to its source. David Icke has done a phenomenal (**Angelic,** to use what I would call **Freeman's** *accurate* appraisal of Icke's accomplishments) job of it on his web site, in his books, and DVDs. The Sun, especially the "Rising Sun" has been used by the same subtle and not-so-subtle forces throughout history that inserted "Father" into our collective understanding of the infinite "One." Jordan Maxwell, on his web site, offers a DVD in which he exposes "The Dawn Of A New Day" for the horrific, hellish, "New World Order" agenda it is. Jordan Maxwell has spent his life researching and exposing this. If you watch the interview with him on the "Project Camelot" web site, you'll realize that he, along with so many others; have been guided by their awareness of their infinite and eternal connection with the Divine. Michael Tsarion and Freeman also have extraordinarily prolific and, from my perspective, authentic, exposes on their web sites, books and DVDs. Matthew Delooze, in his book "Is It Me For A Moment?" exposes the Rising Son Bunch in a very tangible way.

People all over the world associate New Orleans with Mardi Gras or Fat Tuesday. This is the celebrated Bacchanalian holiday observed on the last day before the Christian season of Lent, in which participants give up some form of Earthly pleasure such as eating meat, drinking, or smoking. ***I'm suggesting that in the song, "The House Of The Rising Sun", New Orleans represents Earthbound (as in enslaved) Humanity and that the "House" called the Rising Sun represents us, trapped of our own free will, in a dualistic hell of our own making because of our spiritually blind subservience to The Rising Son Bunch.***

Dave Van Ronk

The House of The Rising Sun

There is a house in New Orleans

They call the Rising Sun

It's been the ruin of many a poor boy

And God, I know I'm one.

My mother was a tailor

She sewed my new blue jeans

My father was a gamblin' man

Way down in New Orleans.

The only thing a gambler needs

is a suitcase and a trunk

and the only time he'll be satisfied

is when he's on a drunk.

I've got one foot on the platform

The other foot on the train

I'm going back to New Orleans

To wear that ball and chain.

So mothers tell your children

Not to do what I have done

Spend your life in sin and misery

In the House of the Rising Sun.

One of the broad spectrum of examples of speaking in tongues is what happens daily on "kids" TV shows such as "The Simpsons", "Southpark", and "Sponge-Bob Square Pants." As with most Television commercials, speaking in tongues may not be of any benefit to the listener unless the listener can correctly interpret what is being communicated to the subconscious and to what purpose. It's my observation that the song, "The House Of The Rising Sun" has a much more profound meaning than the one taken at face value, which kind of reminds me of "Humpty Dumpty." It was so tragic, what happened, forever and ever.

The "Face Value" interpretation goes something like this: The House in New Orleans called "the Rising sun" is a whorehouse with a bar and a casino. The singer is relating his tragic life story as the son of a good and loving mother who worked hard to provide for him, and a deadbeat, shiftless, alcoholic father, who gambles for a living. The son didn't listen to his mother, and followed his father's example of gambling, womanizing, and drinking. It caught up with him and now he's going to spend the rest of his life in a New Orleans's jail.

Here's My Interpretation:

Baron Guy De Rothschild

David Rockefeller

Queen Elizabeth II & Prince Phillip

From Skull & Bones To the Vatican. An uneasy alliance over Humanity

Big Daddy with his 2 boys W, and Slick Willy, at Santa Clause's Funeral

"Keep the gun in your pants or I'll send you to my wife's clinic. Heh, heh, heh."

President Gerald Ford with his Chief of Staff, Donald Rumsfeld and his Deputy Chief of Staff, Dick Cheney. You can read all about Gerald's meteoric rise to Commander in Chief from the Michigan Mob, to chairing the Warren Commission, to becoming an unelected President, in Cathy O'Brien's book "Transformation of America." She knows these guys in the "Biblical" sense. You may want to adjust your image of the valiant warrior.

The literal interpretation of the ancient astrological Christ Mythos

relating to the Winter Solstice.

The figurative interpretation of the literal interpretation of the ancient Christ mythos concerning Christmas Day and Easter.

Japanese Flag

Tibetan Flag

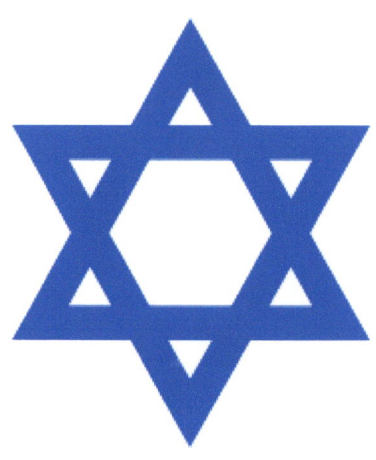

Flag of Israel

Nazi Flag

Maltese Cross

What's *that*

smell?

The usual suspects

The Dynamic Duo

Barackhenaten & Apophis

Aten....Hut!

Amen Ra

Prince William of Wales (William Arthur Phillip Louis; born 21 June 1982), The Summer Solstice, When the sun is most high

William at 21 at the 21st Scout Jambouree

William with his dad upon becoming the 1,000th member of the Order of the Garter. He'll be 30 on the Summer Solstice in 2012.

Just in time for the Summer Olympics which will be held in London that year in a complex that cryptically spells out the word Zion. The mythological Christ began his ministry at 30. What a coincidence!

See if you can spot the Swastika & the Celtic cross in the following symbol.

NATO

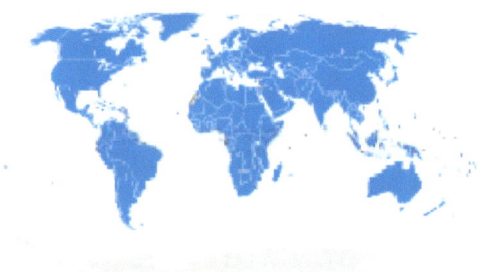

The United Nations

The Federal Reserve, Private, International, Central, Bank

From Big Bro to Big SIS

It *is* a small world after all. Thanks Uncle Walt!

The CIA, Mossad, MI5, & MI6

"The House" Is The Establishment, (the Nephilim) Illuminati, (Elite Secret Societies) who've supplied us with our economically controlling, bloodline hierarchy, our central banking system based on debt, our education system, our medical system, our political system, our leaders, and of course, our Religions.

"The Rising Sun" or **"Risen Son"** is their symbol. It's an inauthentic hijacking of ancient esoteric knowledge. The sun is symbolic of your heart, (As above, so below) your spiritual guidance system. The Christ is a metaphor for your heart, your energetic internal truth discerner, authentically linking you with all that is; spiritually (infinite and eternal) (your upper three Chakras), with all that is; physically (time and space) (your lower three Chakras). By allowing ourselves to be manipulated into taking the metaphor literally, we've disconnected ourselves from our individual authentic sovereignty through the heart and conditioned ourselves to be left-brained egomaniacs with inferiority complexes or bi-polar sheep, born guilty, and with an insatiable desire to be loved and saved. In that way we've become an energetic resource (Human Resources) for an inauthentic hierarchy that is clearly run by the intellectually and technologically brilliant but spiritually insane entities we've been taught are demonic; Satan.

New Orleans represents the Earth.

The singer is "Mankind." (Our language is programmed with sexual bias, which has devastating effects on Humanity, both men and women.)

The Mother is the intuitive (right brained) aspect of the Human condition.

The Father is the linear, five sense, (left brained) ego of the Human condition.

Mankind (Men and Women) has become stuck in its left brain through conditioning and indoctrination. *We've become enslaved to addictions, especially Religion and Money: the biggest faith based addictions – in which the spiritual is manipulated to be seen as separate and own-able.* "You are bought with a price." – The Bible

Sex has been extremely effective in keeping mankind enslaved because through Religion and social mores, we've been conditioned not to pay attention to the esoteric principle. This is similar to taking Newton's Law: "For every action there's an equal and opposite reaction", and saying it's really: "For every action there's a massive reaction that really hits the nail on the head, gets the job done, and puts the original action to shame."

The references to his father only needing a suitcase and a trunk and only being satisfied when he's on a drunk are especially poignant. *This refers to the state that Humanity now finds itself in, of existing to feed its addictions and feeding its addictions in order to exist.* The movie "Up In The Air" with George Clooney is an excellent example. He plays a man whose sister's marriage triggers a spiritual awakening that he's allowed himself to sell his soul for a bogus goal of being the seventh person in history to rack up 10 million frequent flyer miles, efficiently, without getting saddled with the emotional baggage attending Human relationships. He forgot what he came here to do and became a good-looking biological robot that efficiently and effectively works for a heartless Corporation that feeds on Human suffering. (Go look in the mirror, I'll wait.)

The reference to having one foot on the platform and the other on the train, going back to New Orleans to wear that ball and chain is referring to Mankind (men and women) being trapped dimensionally, into reincarnating over and over on a prison planet in which we've become voluntarily enslaved due to our inability to be true to ourselves and consciously participate in our birth visions when we incarnate.

We've been taught that we're eternal beings by our Religions and more subtly by Hollywood where the Priest giving Last Rites to the condemned murderer says, "...and may God have mercy on your eternal soul." Somehow we've allowed ourselves to subconsciously believe that eternity begins when we die physically. How insane is that? There is no beginning. There is no end.

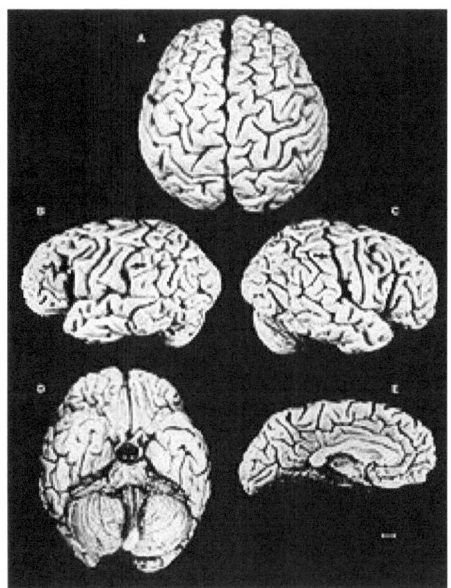

Time, like our left brain, pickled in a jar in a laboratory by itself, exactly like Einstein's brain actually, is finite and exists as an illusion within the infinite and eternal which is the truth.

God is not some separate monstrous Dr. Jekyll and Mr. Hyde, creating spiritual beings with a beginning and no end, who, based on their behavior in this dimension, will merit either everlasting torture or eternal paradise upon their eventual physical demise. Who dreams up this stuff, and why? These are both questions which, if looked at seriously point directly to the source of Mankind's enslavement. Cui Bono? Who benefits from us believing as we've done, that we're ordinary men and women in the street, in need of a savior to redeem us from our deserved eternal torment? Follow the money.

How many ordinary men and women in the street do you know of that could announce to the world the day before 9/11/2001, that they couldn't account for over 2 TRILLION dollars they'd been entrusted with, and not only get away with it, - go on and appropriate more in the form of unfunded debt and take the most powerful nation on Earth into two wars of aggression against international laws that we helped formulate?

God knows it's time we started paying attention to what we believe because it's through what others are telling us to believe that we're creating this nightmarish existence.

We've become so blind to our manipulation and our responsibility for our actions that we've actually allowed the ones who conspired to, and pulled off, the terrorist events known as 9/11, to remove our Constitution and replace it with the torturous Patriot Act, Homeland Security, and Network Television. We've given the ones who brought the world 9/11 and the global military atrocities to follow, carte blanche, to fund wars and create conflict between the greater nations of the world over ideological nonsense made up by elite think tanks, delivered as truth by mainstream news, subtly amplified by Hollywood, and driven home by Goldman Sachs and the Federal Reserve Bank. When someone steps up to confront the insanity, we, the conditioned herd, join the manipulators in condemning our would-be liberators. The time is coming when everyone will be able to see through the manipulation. That's why war and disease are so popular with these lunatics. They intend to reduce the world's population by over 90% in the next few years. This is all commonly understood policy in Brotherhood organizations such as The Council On Foreign Relations, The Bilderberg Group, The Trilateral Commission, and The Club of Rome. They advertize it on the Georgia Guide Stones and in their

"White Papers." Zbigniew Brzezinski, Henry kissinger, and David Rockefeller are on record promoting this treasonous, insane, and hateful agenda.

When one of the players responsible for discerminating retrieved Alien technology (Colonel Philip J. Corso) to the corporate world, to reverse engineer, patent and market to the public, writes a book about it, naming names and providing provable documentation, meaning, in today's 'National Security World', it was all vetted at the highest levels, and the percieved Government and mainstream news media continue to treat the subject like Santa Claus and the Tooth Fairy, an intuitive person begins to discern that what is portrayed as truth by the Church, the Government, and the news media is simply manipulation on a grand scale. The book is "The Day After Roswell." Like Rupert Murdoch advertizes in "The X-Files" *the truth is out there.* This is what is meant when so-called scripture refers to people preferring the lie to the truth……**That's the idea**! They're out to hang us with our own beliefs…………which they gave us.

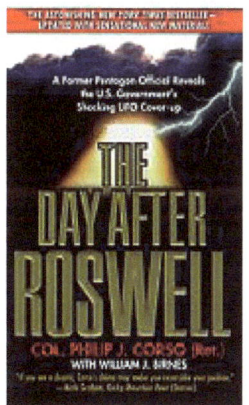

The House of The Rising Sun has made Prostitutes, Addicts, and Gamblers out of all of us………..On Purpose! We sell our souls to a fictitious god whose priests have convinced us we deserve eternal damnation from birth. If you have any concept of what "eternal" means, you can begin to grasp the complete insanity of this doctrine. This is not to imply that God does not exist. Your existance is evidence of God. Your mind is a tool to be used by your heart. Your mind is not equipped to be in the driver's seat, that's the heart's job. Your mind exists from and within God….not outside of God, silly. God is everything. Don't use your mind to separate yourself from her, she may let you do it, because it's through your beliefs that he creates. It's more than likely how we've manifested this false "reality" where money has become our de facto "God." Beginning to attract the awareness of paradox into your life? We're addicted to these religions and in denial of our true infinite and eternal nature. We're in denial of our true nature as powerful co-creators of our own reality. I've heard many spiritually blind, deaf, and dumb, "Gurus" in 12 Step Programs preach that "The only thing you need to know about God is that you ain't him!" As long as you believe that you're your ego, that's fairly accurate, after that it drops like a misogynous turd in the punchbowl of Spiritual Awareness. We've been "programmed" with a false concept of authentic divinity. We accept someone else's concept of God as an old man with a long white beard because it seems to be the popular consensus. After all, Michelangelo was very talented and the Church was very powerful. *We bet against ourselves using our souls as collateral!*

This is deep sorcery. Where does it come from? Who does it to us? We do it to ourselves because we're afraid. We aren't afraid of what Billy Graham thinks of us or what Barrack Obama thinks of us. We're afraid of what our mother will think, or what our teachers will think, or what the guys are going to think. *We've been conditioned like Pavlov's dogs to dance to the consensus trance and teach everyone else the same.* The thought police are in our heads and if we follow our hearts there will be hell to pay. We preach "Give me liberty or give me death" in our elementary schools and "Live Free or Die" but in reality we sell our freedom to those we're afraid have the real power in exchange for the ability to **fit in** with the least amount of molestation.

The Manipulatte

The Illuminati is what the brazen "House Of The Rising Son" bloodline "elite" call themselves. I call them "The Rising Son Bunch"……… when I'm feeling charitable. They've infiltrated the world's secret societies and covertly run the world's "intelligence" agencies. For validation of these seemingly preposterous statements I refer to the works of David Icke, Jordan Maxwell, Freeman, Michael Tsarion, Dr. Steven Greer, Kerry Cassidy, and Bill Ryan. Each of these individuals has more than validated the outside-the-box facts that I'm using to tell this story. The total tonnage of validation of these things available to those who are waking up today is staggering. I'm not trying to convince people of anything. I'm just speaking my truth to those who would listen. For those who are new to this information, if you can read it with an open mind, you'll find this book is really about healing our shattered Human psyche from the inside out. The Rising Son Bunch has been using false education, false government, false medicine, and false spirituality, under the guise of religion to disconnect us from our authentic internal compass, our heart. Through a false economic system based on money as debt and a false spirituality that's disconnected us from our hearts and left us believing we're just our egos, in need of a savior, we've become our own judge, jury, executioner, & slave driver playing a cosmic game of musical chairs for the Rising Son Bunch, vying with each other to get one of the few chairs left when the music stops for the last time. We're learning the art of discerning with our hearts. It's what we were born to do. It's what Bill Wilson did when he found another Alcoholic to help after hearing Death, dressed up as his lover and savior, call to him from the bar one dismal night in Akron, Ohio in 1935. He'd had what's come to be known as a spiritual awakening.

The "Great Ventriloquist" holds up his puppet, the "Great (Howdy Doody) Communicator", for reporters at the White House.

George H. W. Bush is a prime example of the Illuminati. They're not what they appear to be. They're behind all of our religions and "isms" such as: Communism, Socialism, Capitalism, Despotism, and Nepotism. So, of course they're the motivating force behind Corporatism, a happy name for Fascism. They understand what we would call the diseased nature of all of them and use them as mind pattern programming to funnel large groups of people into willingly giving their power to them at a spiritual level. They are behind drug epidemics and the "War on Drugs" bizarrely enough, for the same reasons. Alcoholism is just another ism that they thrive on at our expense. Polarity and duality is a construct they use for control through perception. The black and white square tiles on the floors of their temples represent this concept. The black squares mean "we control all that is wrong, all that is unjust and all that is unfair." The white squares mean "We control all that is Right, all that is just, and all that is fair." They control through "divide and conquer." Through our education, we're taught to believe things like, "Democracy equals freedom." Fifty-one people telling forty-nine people what to do is not freedom. We've been conditioned to see things in polarities; Democrat, Republican, left, right, right, wrong, male, female. These are then played off against each other so we stay in the victim or victor mentality. This is amplified and glorified through competetive sports, which is perceived as being just next to cleanliness when it comes to godliness.

"I did not have sex with that woman"

The thing about the Rising Son Bunch is that they've had one ultimate goal since the dawn of recorded history. This is why we've been taught to have so much admiration for Alexander the Great, Ghengis Khan, and Vlad the

Impaler. That goal, just like the cartoon "Pinky and the Brain" used to suggest at the end of every episode, is complete world domination, a global fascist dictatorship, or as George H. W. himself put it, before Congress, on 9/11/1991: a **New World Order**. This is symbolized presently in both houses of the U.S. Congress and on the back of the dime by the Fasci. On the back of the dollar bill, it's the "E Pluribus Unum" and the "Novus Ordo Seclorum."

Out of many; One   **New World Order**

The Fasci (literally Latin for fagot) are a bundle of sticks signifying "we the People" tied together and ruled from the top with an axe head of iron. The Rising Son Gang has used the same occult methods for achieving their goals since the "dawn" of recorded history. I was born in the Belgian Congo. It was called that because the Rising Son Bunch from Belgium had bullied, raped, and pillaged their way, in the name of Leopold, their King, oh, and let's not forget, "God", into a position of national domination, euphemistically referred to as colonization. One of their favorite methods of achieving and maintaining control is to play the indigenous people off against each other. In Congo, that would be the Tutsis and the Hutus. The Tutsis are quite tall and have produced some exceptional basketball players, not to mention, a few radical dance maneuvers (the Watutsi). The Belgian Rising Son bunch would put them in powerful positions in government and commerce over the Hutus who were shorter, bush people, whose cousins have starred in movies like the very appropriately named, "The Gods Must Be Crazy." The Hutus, as you might imagine, were absolutely thrilled with this new caste system they found themselves at the bottom of. After being amply supplied with machetes and alcohol by the Rising Son Boys, the Hutus would surprize the Tutsis with a late-night drunken decapitation party using the time-honored, cart-before-the- horse "lets get hammered and level the playing field" method.

This event goes down in Tutsiland like 9/11 with *really big* box-cutters. There will be retribution. These wars are still going on today with weapons, technical know-how, and the *debt* to buy them with, amply supplied by the Risen Son Brigade with the addition of biological warfare, known as AIDS, thrown in as a gift. The arms and medicine are paid for with blood diamonds, uranium, and many other minerals and resources with which select corrupt Congolese make themselves exponentially more powerful than their brothers (see **Mobutu**). This method of getting what they want by subtly playing one side off against the other is known as the *Hegelian Dialectic*.

Cause the problem, blame someone else, offer the solution.

David Icke calls it Problem, Reaction, Solution. You know the Congolese don't want to work like dogs mining the purest (radioactive) uranium in the world that will be used in the bombs dropped on Hiroshima and Nagasaki and has been laying peacefully for thousands of years buried underground in their country, so you use economic and social mores to create an imbalance among the locals. In no time you're selling guns and armored vehicles to the chiefs on both sides and paying cheap rates for all the labor you need to mine minerals that are meant to be used to bring the world to its knees in front of the beast; The New World Order.

The Hegelian Dialectic is occultically symbolized, all over the world, by the double-headed Eagle.

Problem, Reaction, Solution

When Karl Marx wrote about Thesis, Anti-thesis, Synthesis, he was describing *this* methodology. People are never going to knowingly and willingly give up their authentic wealth, resources, and energy to a small group of nasty tyrants who enjoy inflicting pain and suffering. To accomplish this they have to cause a problem and blame someone else for it, exactly like what happened at Oklahoma City and on 9/11. Misdirection is their thing and since they control all the Network News, Newspapers, Periodicals, as well as the world economy through central banks, it's not difficult for them to program our thoughts with lies. Shucks, they pay us, **the little guys**, to do it for them, with *our* money. When these horrific events happen, the people say, "This can't go on!" This is always followed by, as David Icke says, (giving our power away) "What are *they* going to do about it?" The "Authorities" then step in and offer the solution *they* wanted in the first place.

Iraqi Oil Fields http://www.businessinsider.com/investing-in-iraq-oil-fields-2010-4 & Baku, the largest city in Azerbaijan, on the Caspian Sea. The Caspian Basin is worth an estimated $12 trillion in Petro$ alone. With inflation, roll dice & multiply.

This is how Communism came to be what it is. This is what Socialism is all about and sadly, as many Americans are waking up to, this is what Capitalism, or as it has turned out to be, Corporatism, is all about. It's just the Rising Son

Bunch covertly manipulating their New World Order into place. On 9/11, when the Rising Sun Gang, who is not representative of a single Country, but manipulates them all, brought down the World Trade Center and blamed it on 19 indestructable passport and bandana owning, Keystone Cop-flying, pork eating, womanizing, coke snorting, alcoholic, **Muslim Fundamentalists** with *box cutters*, who "*hated us for our freedom*", controlled from a cave in Afghanistan by a very tall diabetic CIA Asset on dialisis, code named Tim Osman,……….

(AKA Usama binBoogyman, speaks from the grave:

"I have already said that I am not involved in the 11 September attacks in the United States. As a Muslim, I try my best to avoid telling a lie. I had no knowledge of these attacks, nor do I consider the killing of innocent women, children and other humans as an appreciable act. Islam strictly forbids causing harm to innocent women, children and other people. Such a practice is forbidden even in the course of a battle."
Osama Bin Laden (from a Pakistan Karachi Ummat news interview suppressed in the U.S. and Britian – September 28, 2001)

"Bin Laden has not been formally charged in connection to 9/11."
FBI Operative Rex Tomb (Chief of Investigative Publicity at the FBI speaking for the Justice Department. 6/5/2006)

http://homelessonthehighdesert.wordpress.com/2008/05/28/cia-agent-tim-osman/)

…….that was a prime example of the cynically, ludicrously liberal, use of the Hegelian Dialectic in action. The Illuminati have grown fat and sassy on how ridiculously easy it is for them to manipulate Humanity. They wanted Helen Keller to be able to see through this eventually. It's part of their religion. That's part of the message with this one. It's like Dick Cheney getting drunk, shooting an aging lawyer in the face and making him apologize for it on

National Television when the news finally gets out 3 days after the fact. It's like the people's comedian, Jon Stewart, who easily and publicly walks us through the ridiculous shenanigans Cheney gets away with, but can't smell a Zionist gatekeeper wearing his own 9 year old underwear when it comes to 9/11 Red Herrings. Cheney could have shot a six year old girl in front of the White House on National Television, live, and it would have been her fault. What are you going to do about it? Call the Washington Post? The FBI? The CIA? That's what they're saying. "Who ya goona call?" Jesus? Ghost-Busters?

This book is about helping those who are ready - to make the connection between **Addictions** and……….**Politics, Money, and…..RELIGION**.

Politics, Money, and Religion are all Addictions the Illuminati have been using to keep us consciously disconnected from *infinite consciousness, which is what we are*. **Thank you, David Icke**. Addictions are what we've been conditioned to turn to when the pain of remaining present and conscious in this dimension feels overwhelming. **Ian Xel Lundgold** does an incredible job of revealing this also in his presentation about the Mayan Calendar. If you're hungry to get up to speed with this information, simply google his name and watch the presentation. It's packed with High-Energy information critical to our times.

9/11, who would conceive of such a dispicably twisted thing and actually pull it off on live television? Abu Ghraib, who would concieve of such a dispicably twisted thing and then get the pictures plastered on international television and in time magazine? Anyone who's served in the Military knows that was no accident. Extraordinary rendition, who would conceive of such a horrendously dispicable thing and then brag about it in the International Press? Why? How could 9/11 have been carried out with the multiply redundant security measures that have been in place to prevent exactly those types of scenarios from ever taking place?

Before the collective subconsciousness had time to grasp what was entailed in symbollically flying two planes full of passengers into the Boaz and Jachin phallic symbols of American economic prowess…using box-cutters……

…before the collective consciousness had time to grasp what is really entailed in symbollically flying a plane load of "innocent" passengers into the one recently re-fortified wall at the Pentagon, the world's most secure building, using box-cutters……

……before the collective superconsciousness had successfully communicated what had to be involved in symbolically flying a plane load of magic phone owning patriots straight into the ground, we were told Uncle Sherlock Holmes Sam had already figured it all out.

Chairman of the Joint Chiefs Richard Myers /Seal of the Federal Aviation Administration

It was 19 Muslim Fundamentalists with box-cutters who hated us for our freedom, yeah that's the ticket, everybody said so. It's just that up until it happened, none of our high tech, multi-trillion dollar misplacing, black budgeted, agencies ever would have guessed or had a clue about it. Yeah, that's the ticket, everybody said so. Quite a while after the President had been notified by his Chief of Staff, Andy Card, (What a Card!) while reading "My Pet Goat" with the Knights Templar (Baphomet) illiterate ……

Second Graders in Florida, that the Nation was under attack, these suicidal, technological wonder, Islamic, flyboys got the Pentagon to stand down using box-cutters. Yeah, that's clearly what happened! You can take that to the bank. The Pentagon did! The White House Did! Congress did! Fox News did! NBC, ABC, CBS, CNN, and the History Channel did! The Crème de la Crème was how in the (Mossad) world they ever got Building Seven of the World Trade Center, which housed Giuliani's Command and Control Center, to fall neatly into it's own footprint at free fall speed twenty minutes after the BBC had announced, surprise, that it had fallen, *without box-cutters this time*, and then got the 9/11 Investigation Committee, guided by Philip Zelikow, with his degree in **Social Engineering and the book he co-wrote with Condoleezza Rice**, to completely overlook those amazing facts. The whole purpose of the 9/11 Investigation Committee, as far as we, the people, knew, was to find the truth, not hide it. But hey, that's what happened. You can look it up. Don't forget your box-cutters and your Koran. We will not forget. Support our troops.

Chapter Four

The Profound Importance Of Being True To Yourself

It's All About The O 1...

(The Divine Order Of Everything)

The Serenity Meditation

I Am The Serenity That Is From Being Infinite & Eternal Consciousness, The Courage To Create Authentically From That Awareness, & Wisdom To Be True To Myself While Showing Reverence And Respect For My Infinite Reflections In This World.

The Subtle Differences Between Arrogance And Humility

Tom Brokaw

Hunter S. Thompson

Hunter S. Thompson, who made a good living documenting life from the perspective of a practicing alcoholic and drug addict made note of a quote by a man he calls Dr. Johnson; "He who makes a beast of himself gets rid of the pain of being a man." In case anyone is assuming I'm using Hunter as an example of arrogance as compared with humility, I am not. Hunter, in my opinion, was a high profile example of the millions of people with marvelous intellects and an authentic motivation to be true to themselves, who find the path of the practicing addict an authentic mirror of the Human condition.

The reason addictions are such a common aspect of the Human condition is that they allow us to survive and even enjoy conditions in which we feel trapped and powerless. Tom Brokaw comes to mind. I get the feeling he's survived and even enjoyed his role as brown-noser of the "Greatest Generation." I think Tom, because of his blood more than likely, is privy to a subtler form of getting rid of the pain of being a man that actually has more to do with possession. In order to break free of the slavery to addictions of which we've all fallen victim, we need to attract into our conscious awareness a deeper understanding of the word "Humility." I've found the writings of Bill Wilson to be divinely inspired on many more than a dozen occasions. On page 58 of his book "Twelve Steps And Twelve Traditions", he gives what to me, is an authentic, divinely inspired, definition of the word.

Bill Wilson

Humility – it amounts to the clear recognition of who and what we really are, followed by the sincere desire to become what we could be. In the context of the book it's clear that what Bill is consciously referring to are our defects of character, which, at that point in the book, we're in the process of confessing to God, to ourselves, and another Human Being. Like "Humpty

Dumpty" and "The House Of The Rising Sun", there's a deeper meaning, which once understood, brings a great deal more clarity, comfort, and peace. The whole purpose of the Twelve Steps is to spark a spiritual awakening, which Wilson became aware was his only chance of transcending the "Disease" of Alcoholism. **He had one**.

Synchronistically, it was exactly the kind of **"Psychic Change"** that **Carl Jung** described to his patient **Rowland Hazard**, who had sought his advice regarding alcoholism. Rowland returned to America and joined the Oxford Group in an effort to spark a 'Psychic Change." One of the principles they were using to "cure" diseases they had determined were **spiritual** in nature was to work intensively with others who were similarly afflicted.

Rowland Hazard   **Carl Jung**

After Bill had his **"White Light"** experience he never drank again. He used the spiritual principles of the Oxford Group to ensure his sobriety. He and the group of alcoholics he began working with developed the Twelve Steps for this purpose. The whole purpose of the Twelve Steps was to spark **a spiritual awakening**. Once we're spiritually cognizant, it becomes obvious that *"What" we are is Spiritual Beingness, infinite and eternal. "Who" we are has to do with our "Birth Vision"* within the matrix of physicality, which has to do with an awareness of Astrology, the moment we started breathing oxygen on our own, and our geographic location on the Earth. We are purposely not taught these things because it has to do with authentic power. The Rising Son Bunch holds all the aces as long as we believe we're playing poker.

The purpose of doing a Fourth and Fifth Step is to become conscious physically and mentally of the fears that motivate all our defects of character. We *are not* those defects of character. If we can be made to believe that we're broken, small, powerless, bad, sinful, etc. we'll be motivated by the fears that naturally support those beliefs and continue to manifest a victim or victor reality. In that state of mind, addiction retains its power over us and we'll either find another addiction or relapse.

We've been conditioned not to recognize Religion as an addiction. For this reason Religions are one of the biggest addictions and most successful forms of mind control the world has ever seen. Do you think Christianity's powerful? Flip that coin over and have a look at the 13 Satanic families really running the world because of our collective denial. Thank you Mick Jagger. By marrying Religion with Money "In God We Trust", the Rising Son Bunch has subconsciously conditioned us to voluntarily sell ourselves spiritually, one moment at a time, to them, because we actually believe they're better than us. Through Religions and finance we can join the consensus trance that we're all just ordinary men and women in the street. We're born sinners deserving everlasting punishment. God has blessed the Rothschilds, The Windsors, the Rockefellers, the Bushes, Bill Gates, Rupert Murdoch, Dick Cheney, Donald Rumsfeld, Condoleezza Rice, and Barack Obama. If you work hard and serve "Him", "He" will bless you too! Twelve Step **Programs** have become another Religion with personality cults galore and co-dependant cliques just like all religions. Hunter Thompson was not accidentally a practicing alcoholic and drug addict. At this point it's critical to remember not to throw the Baby out with the Bathwater. The breakthrough in spiritual awareness Bill Wilson is responsible for is undeniable and authentic. It's been hi-jacked just like spiritual awareness always has, through religion.

The energy of spirit is Love. That's **what** we are. Through our thoughts it can be slowed way down to what we emotionally call fear. Fear is useful as a point of reference and contrast to guide us back to the higher vibrational emotional state. When we make fear our God, we worship ruthlessness and hope. When we feel powerless we look for and count on a savior. Instead of recognizing our own infinite and eternal authenticity and seeing it in each other, we've allowed ourselves to become a resource (Human Resources) for Corporatism, which is just another name for Nazi Germany or Fascist Italy. This is the message mankind has been getting loud and clear since the advent of nuclear weaponry. **Responsible people do not wage war**. *War is a racket*. The Rising Son Bunch have been manipulating humanity into wars they never wanted for thousands of years and glorifying them. They've gotten us to identify with them and take pride in being violent warriors. This is insane. It's like taking pride in being a child molester. Infinite Love is the only Truth, everything else is illusion. Follow that with the sincere desire to become what you could be and you've nailed the authentic purpose for your physical existence. **Be True To Yourself.** *It ain't easy!* When we look outside ourselves for validation, and we're holding fear inside, we attract the validation of those fears from the outside. The outer world or physical is a manifestation of the inner world, or spiritual.

Psychic sovereignty – Putting It All Back Together

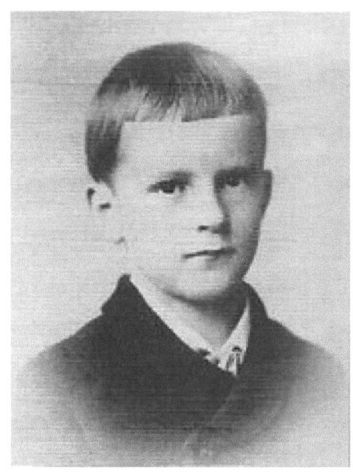

Carl Jung at age 6

The Risen Son Brigade thrives on keeping us distracted and frightened. This is why the Serenity Prayer is so important to recovering alcoholics. Alcoholics need to find a spell, mantra, or incantation they can successfully use to quiet the cacophony of voices screaming for attention from their DNA. The Serenity Prayer is such a device. As we continue to awaken spiritually, we begin to discern the programming in the Serenity Prayer from the perspective of awareness. We've been conditioned to see ourselves as separate from God. We've been programmed to petition an external "God" for something that's innately "Ours" via an incantation of an authentic understanding of the Divine order of things. "Serenity to accept the things I cannot change" is the Divine Feminine Principle or Holy Spirit Consciousness, present in both men and women. "Courage to change the things I can" is the Divine Masculine Principle or Creative consciousness, present in both men and women. The "Wisdom to know the difference" comes naturally with an authentic understanding of

Humility – The clear recognition of <u>who</u> and <u>what</u> you really are, <u>followed</u> by the <u>sincere</u> desire to become what you could be. In other words – **to create authentically in the physical world from the awareness of Divine spiritual Integrity or "Love." This has always been symbolized esoterically by the point within the circle.**

Bill Wilson, Carl Jung, and Reinhold Neibuhr who is credited with the Serenity Prayer were each conveying their perspectives of how supremely important the Truth is. The Truth Is. The Truth is not validated by the amount of people voting for it or invalidated by the amount of people who don't see it. The Truth Is. The ancients knew this and taught it. The word "Is" is a sygil for the Egyptian goddess Isis, as is the Dollar sign "$". Isis was the Virgin Mother, the Divine Feminine. The Rising Son Bunch from back in the time of the Pharoah, Akhenaton, (Moses?) pulled this knowledge from the public and established the House of The Rising Sun which we've come to know as the Establishment. David Icke had a spiritual awakening about 20 years ago and began revealing the Truth. He was a Proffessional Soccer Player, not an alcoholic. It didn't matter. The Truth got his attention through the pain of Rheumatoid Arthritis. By following his heart and being True to himself he shattered the false eggshell that "all the Kings' horses and all the kings' men" had imprisoned him (& us) in. We've been creating an inauthentic illusory world for the benefit of some very sick twisted entities that are in this world and of this world, out of fear of an inauthentic god. Spiritual awakening is about resonating with the Truth. Infinite Love is the only Truth, everything else is illusion.

If you continue to perceive yourself as a born sinner, or a broken personality, as we've been heavily programmed to do (The Weakest Link), you'll continue to manifest the need for a savior, which is exactly what the Hegelian Dialectic of the Risen Son Bunch is all about. They've got something for you. It's a microchip. They expect you'll be begging for it.

When Humpty Dumpty Hatched

It's only through our choosing to remain ignorant of these symbols that a Corporate Department Store named Target has been able to appropriate the symbol of Unity Consciousness, color it bright red, like an outrageous pornagraphic representation of the Divine Union at the Root Chakra and sell it to us like we're in agreement with them or something. In my humble opinion, Hunter Thompson was not accidentally an alcoholic and a drug addict, and he was more spiritually aware than most "Christians." "Fear and Loathing In Las Vegas"....no kiddin' huh? Alcoholism is one of the many addictions that are now triggering an awareness in Humanity that we've been profoundly asleep spiritually by design. We have Bill Wilson and Carl Jung to thank for cognitively connecting disease, addiction, and spirituality in the collective consciousness. Until Bill came along and divined the anonymous fellowship of A.

A. through synchronicity and being true to himself, alcoholics were a pretty helpless bunch in this world. By the time it was determined we were alcoholic, we were for the most part, in the chronic phase of the disease. Mark Twain came close to summing up religion's attitude towards alcoholism in "Huckleberry Finn" when the Reverend who tried to reform Huck's Dad said, "You might be able to reform him with a shotgun, but I doubt it." Psychiatry was on the road towards defining alcoholism as a valium or quaalude deficiency in individuals whose parents were the usual suspects.

Dayton Ohio Members, 1942

Members wore masks: to protect their anonymity, members of the Dayton, Ohio, AA chapter donned masks while posing for the press in 1942.

Anonymity & Paradox

Anonymity is another one of those spiritual principles that seems to mean one thing when you're first introduced, and eventually is perceived as exactly the opposite. I've known my last name was **Prester** for most of my life and yet for most of that time I've had few clues as to what or who I really was. Spiritual awareness is realizing that just because you know someone's last name, their gender, date of birth, health, work, and criminal records doesn't mean you really have a clue what or who they really are. Certain individuals in the alphabet soup of black budget agencies surrounding Washington D. C. are very sensitive to that bit of information. This is why biometrics and the Alice in Wonderland technology in use by Homeland Security and the Pentagram, er, I mean Pentagon has grown exponentially over the last decade. It has nothing to do with protecting you from "terrorists" like they pretend. It's about being able to maintain control over people who are waking up spiritually and preventing others from ever waking up. When I say "my name is --- and I'm an alcoholic", I'm not telling you what I am or who I am, I'm just identifying the common disease that triggered my awareness that I needed to wake up spiritually or lose my ability to authentically manifest in this dimension. I am not that disease, capiche? When I say, "my name is --- and I'm an alcoholic", you may think you know what I'm talking about, but unless you're an alcoholic yourself, you have no clue. It's like saying E= MC squared. You may recognize the formula and connect it with Einstein's theory of relativity, but until you've done the math, it's just someone else's good idea. We live in a society where acknowledging the truth is a fool's game in the collective unconsciousness, and yet we pretend that we're in agreement that we're only as sick as our secrets and the best of us tell the truth all the time. We're all aware to a degree that our governments lie to us all the time and that our judicial system has basically come down to who owns the judge or who can afford the best lawyer and lawyer is a synonym for high-priced liar. We know that it's the scum that rises to the top because they can be bought but we're afraid of the consequences of acknowledging all of this in our own personal paradigm so we give lip service to the truth, feed the beast, and hope for a savior. The age of innocence is over. The story of Jesus is about you and me. Anonymity is about Unity Consciousness. Anonymity is about Principles before personalities. My personality is simply here to manifest or reveal in the physical our authentic oneness, Anonymity. We are each other. That includes the Illuminati. It doesn't mean we can't think for ourselves or relieve us of the responsibility to be true to ourselves. The Illuminati are in the driver's seat because we put them there. ***Our responsibility now that we know, is to remove them from*** *the driver's seat, lock them up, use their stolen booty to relieve the immediate ongoing suffering, globally, release the suppressed medicinal and energy technology that's supported their tyranny, and hold a well documented, fearless, and thorough investigation so that this kind of sorcery never plagues Humanity again. It's an inside job. Be true to yourself and follow your heart.*

Religions and governments have done a great job convincing people that there is much to fear in spite of FDR's rhetoric to the contrary. Religions have convinced us that "We have met the enemy, and he is us." Governments have convinced us that we need them to protect us from ourselves.

FDR signing the Declaration of War 12/08/1941

This is because we're ignorant of Who and What we are. FEAR is the principle which allows us to remain ignorant of who and what we are – even if it is followed by the sincere desire to become what we could be. If I sincerely believe that I'm a lackey, or in contemporary TV parlance, a slacker, my sincerest desire can only ultimately be to become a better lackey or slacker.

I'm going to let you all in on a little secret. Don't tell anybody, ok? **I'm infinite and eternal consciousness** having an experience in this illusory, finite, physical, world as an African American named Robert Roy Prester. Shhhhhhh. How's that for breaking my anonymity? We have eveything in common with everything, except for the 'experience in this finite, illusory, world' part, which is an illusion as modern quantum physics has proven, upon which we base most of our decisions. FEAR is why we continue to give our authentic spiritual power away to religions and governments and the private international central bankers who own them. Let's not get into who owns *them* right now because **ultimately**, it's us, but let's just say, *"Its ridiculous, what we're doing!"* They supply us with our governments, religions, education, health care, and financial structure. We've got this FEAR and we think it might be legitimate. Paradoxically, we're afraid our FEAR might not be legitimate, so we develop addictions to religions, governments, schools, medicine, and **alcohol** to hedge our bets & as a means of sedating and controlling our spiritual awareness. Along comes a spiritually profound fellowship that transcends religion and psychiatry, which is how GOVERNMENTs have OFFICIALLY dealt with alcoholism in the past, once it was undeniable. Now we, who don't trust our governments, but still suspect fundamentalists with box-cutters of slamming one of our own commercial jets into the most heavily secured building in the world…………………using box-cutters, because the government tells us so, naively assume Alcoholics Anonymous would not be a target…………………………………………………………………………

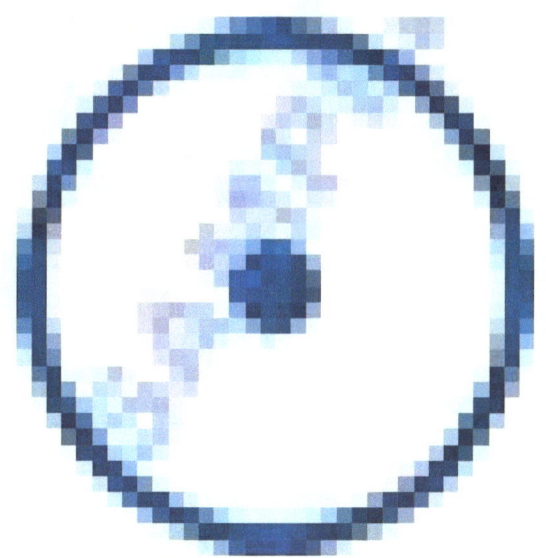

………………………………..for those who've been using their secret knowledge of the Twelve Steps of Horus and the spiritual nature of everything to control and manipulate Mankind. I've got three words to say about that:

You're Getting Sleepy…

Everyone familiar with World War II should, by now have at least a superficial knowledge of the relationship between the Third Reich and the Occult. That's what I'm referring to when I say "those who've been using their secret knowledge of the spiritual nature of everything to control and manipulate Mankind." They didn't just dry up and blow away when Germany fell to the Allies. Germany and the Allies were used, abused, and discarded by these guys. Because we didn't know who and what we are, much less who and what they are, we helped them do it out of FEAR. In Project Paperclip, the best (or worst) Nazi Scientists, including Josef Mengele, and Werner Von Braun were rounded up and snuck (sneaked? Snackered?) into the United States of America to continue their *glorious work*, only now, on our behalf. This has been clearly documented by David Icke, Cathy O'Brien, and Mark Phillips, among many, many, many, others.

Natural Progression

When Wilbur and Orville Wright designed their first airplane – it wasn't an F – 14 Tomcat or a Boing 757. I suspect the same analogy can be applied to the breakthrough in spiritual awareness that attended the anonynous Bill Wilson in developing the Twelve Step Fellowship known as Alcoholics Anonymous. Perceiving the connections to those who manipulate governments and religions through deception, sorcery, and FEAR is critical to understanding what a major threat Alcoholics Anonymous and all twelve Step fellowships are to those who've been using their hidden or "Occult" spiritual knowledge on the puplic in order To maintain Power and control.

John D. Rockefeller, Early AA Advocate

This understanding should make it crystal clear to Christian and non-Christian alike that by closing Twelve Step meetings with a blatantly Christian prayer – we are unconsciously participating in the corruption of our own spiritual awakening. **Religions are divisive by nature**. This is not to suggest that

Christians can't get sober or to ban any religion. The anonymous Dr. Bob Smith died a "sober" Christian Proctologist if that's how you identify a person. By allying ourselves with a religion and closing meetings with "The Lord's Prayer" we manifest that we're incapable of "grasping and developing a manner of living that demands rigorous honesty."

By our fears we've attracted what has become known as the Illuminati (the Rising Son Bunch) and the New World Order (Hell). There's a non-Human element in the hierarchy above them that's been using Humanity like a parasite uses its host. Our FEAR is what has created this hellish agenda. By waking up spiritually, releasing our attachments to our fears, and focusing with integrity on what we truly desire from the heart, we're changing the world. That's what's happening. The Rising Son Bunch has been aware of, and planning for this time for millennia. They know we're waking up to our multi-dimensional, infinite nature, to the fact that we're not alone in the universe, and to the fact that we've been purposely lied to and preyed upon by so-called authority. They rule through fear, and fear and greed are all they know. One of the Rising Son Bunch's great puppets in the last century was FDR. He was famous for saying, "The only thing we have to fear is fear itself." No! That's not it. We don't have to fear, fear itself. *We only need the clear recognition of who and what we really are, followed by the sincere desire to become what we could be*.

"Some even believe we are part of a secret cabal working against the best interests of the United States, characterizing my family and me as 'Internationalists' and of conspiring with others around the world to build a more integrated global political and economic structure – one world, if you will. If that is the charge, I stand guilty, and I am proud of it."

- David Rockefeller in his 2002 memoirs

David Rockefeller (right) and bodyguard James Ford - southern end of Petit Allee Saint-Antoine, Versailles - 17th May 2003.

Hurray For Hollywood

The Rising Son Bunch control the world through mind pattern programming. They use symbolism and thought forms to get Human Beings to do what they want done. Like the black and white floor tiles and Freud's cigars and bananas, everything stands for something else. One of the major exoteric or exposed symbols of the Rising Son Brigade is the pyramid. This stands for the blade or the male principle. You'll find this on top of their obelisks, which symbolize the male phallus, and on top of their church steeples, symbolic of the same thing. The Christmas Tree and Holly Tree symbolize this same geometric shape with the added significance of being born again or resurrection. In the dead of winter these upright triangular shaped trees remain green and vital, signifying life. Green is the color associated with the heart chakra. When a Sorcerer makes a magic wand he uses the wood of the holly, or "Hollywood." They have a habit of surrounding their geomancy (architectural stone devices) like the Georgia Guide Stones with it.

The Georgia Guide Stones

Hollywood is that part of the House of the Rising Son that uses cinematic theater to plant thought forms or cast a spell over the mass consciousness.

Freeman of the Freeman Perspective, Matthew Delooze in his book "Is It Me For A Moment?", Jordan Maxwell, Michael Tsarion, and David Icke all do masterful jobs of exposing how the Illuminati are using Hollywood and the Music Industries to condition and indoctrinate Humanity with thought forms that act like a hypnotic spell. The movie "V For Vendetta" is an example of this. V as in "V"erizon & "VV"ireless symbolizes the esoteric or hidden, female principle. It's the reverse of the male, exoteric, exposed principle as in  or "M"ichael "M"oore of "incredibly-aware-when-it-comes-to-keeping-you-focused-on-politics-and-ideologies" fame. V is what is referred to in the Occult as the "Chalice" or in the Christian Religion, which, a surprise to some, comes from the Occult, as the Holy Grail. Dan Brown has been used to release a bunch of misinformation and disinformation, combined cleverly with fact, in order to suppress and confuse mainstream awareness. In his movie about the Illuminati, Dan Brown's "Angels and Demons", Opie Taylor reveals that they're all just one big happy Illuminati family at the very beginning of the picture by parading the Goddess, Columbia out in front of God and everybody with her torch. In the Christian Religion, her part is played by the Virgin Mary and then later by Mary Magdalene. The illumined founding fathers of the United States encrypted their manipulation of the Christian Religion in the United States themselves by naming the capitol after their Goddess, Columbia, and the two states immediately bordering her, *Virgin*ia and *Mary*land.

What, no all-seeing eye? Wait a minute...

The blade unites with the chalice and creates the whole. The Star of David is but one visual symbol of this union, the compass and square of Freemasonry is another. **Vigilant Citizen** does a superb job on his web site of revealing the connection between Zionism and Freemasonry much to the stunned amazement of most Jews,  Christians, and Freemasons  alike.

http://vigilantcitizen.com/?p=1229

On the surface, "V For Vendetta" seems to be all about exposing the hidden agenda of the fascist elite and getting retribution. It feels so right to those who are aware of the manipulation until Freeman points out the subtle way in which the audience is enticed into endorsing with their hearts, Trauma Based Mind Control to achieve its purposes. "V" being the hidden principle, it also represents 6 or the Christ. In the Occult, VV or 66 represents the Qlippoth or Fallen Angels, the dark side of the tree of Life, whose chief is Lucifer. They are Luciferians, the Light Bringers whose story is told in the mythology of Prometheus, who stole fire from the "gods." Another of their symbols is the torch being held by Columbia. This is the same torch used in the Olympics and as the Eternal Flame on top of JFK's grave in Arlington. It's all analogous to Lucifer or Venus, the goddess of Beauty and Love, the Bright and morning Star. This is how the incredibly aware "V For Vendetta" becomes another subtle form of hypnotic mind control aimed at getting us to voluntarily endorse the very tools they're using to enslave us, such as trauma based mind control. It's like the "Salvation Army" or "Christ for Vendetta."

Sculpture of Prometheus in front of the GE Building at the Rockefeller Center (New York City, New York, United States).

Ideas and phrases like the "War on Drugs" and the "War on Terror" can finally be clearly seen for what they are: Thought Form Programming. Declaring War on Drugs or Terror is an insane thing for Human Beings to even contemplate. **War is Terror. War is a Racket. Declaring war on war is the equivalent of rape for abstinence**. We already learned that Prohibition, besides seriously not working, just makes organized crime powerful enough to put a man in the White House. That man, JFK told the first Presidential model, mind controlled, sex slave, Marilyn Monroe, about extra-terrestrials and the technology we'd gotten from them and, as her programming started to unravel, allegedly having to do with her age, she decided to go public with that information, for which she was terminated. After the Bay of Pigs, JFK realized that he didn't want to take orders from these corrupt Energy Barrons any more and publicly denounced the Illuminati, for which he was terminated.

Declaring war on Drugs or terror is insane. Where is the critical thinking in our "Free Society" that brings this awareness to consciousness? Not on Television. Not in the Newspaper. Not in Church. Not in Twelve Step Programs who have no oppinion on outside issues such as honesty, hallowed be thy name and keep comin' back. Certainly not in school. War is a Racket. This isn't a theory. This isn't the delusional hocus pocus of Bill O' Reilly, Glen Beck, or some "half-baked wing nut." This is the sober, documented, highly motivated conclusion of arguably, the most capable and experienced United States Warrior, ever, after a meritorious lifetime of service. This wasn't written by Ulysses S. Grant who went from Private to Commander in Chief in four years. This is about you being true to yourself. Look up Marine Corps General Smedley Butler and ask yourself if you can think of anyone else who even comes close to being as qualified to write about what war is and is not. This is what spiritual awakening is all about, you being true to yourself. We as a species are attracting the necessary emotional, mental, and physical pain into our lives via the Illuminati's manipulation, to wake us up out of our hypnotic conscensus trance and take a critical look at the sheer tonnage of raw sewage we've been voluntarily endorsing to our own detriment. We're becoming conscious of our personal roles in our own enslavement. We can no longer pretend we don't know better.

When we endorse concepts such as the "War on Drugs" or the "War on Terror" either by active participation or by passively paying taxes to support them and pretending to be powerless – we're just as much to blame as those who fell under the Nazi umbrella in World War II. Hollywood uses movies like "V for Vendetta" to subtly hijack those who are waking up into voluntarily endorsing **"the end justifies the means."**

It doesn't, it never did and it never will. We have to know that as a species before we can move on.

Spelling It Out

When Human Beings realize that they're trapped in an addiction, they become aware that something is going to have to change or they will physically die. This has to do with core beliefs. They become gradually, or sometimes instantly aware that something they're holding to be true or that they love, or that they've unconsciously been giving their power to – is killing them. The vast majority just deny and ignore this "Catch 22" situation, where they feel damned if they do and damned if they don't and eventually die. Those who are able to maintain their connection with the high value the spirit places on physical manifestation begin to entertain the notion that, perhaps there is something else which would allow them to go on physically without this thing that had meant so much to them and was now obviously killing them. This is extremely difficult to do and usually requires a great deal of sustained pain in order to manifest the required motivation and determination to step out into the great wide open in the belief that something better not only exists but will come along in a timely fashion. To me, this is what the Third Step in Twelve Step programs is all about – stepping out into the great wide open in the belief that the spiritual is the causal source not only of our addictions, but of the means to transcend them. This is a belief in a new thought form, a higher vibration. Actually, it's a belief we had abandoned in order to fit in. It's born of a firm belief in the finite that's been shaken to its core and found inadequate. It's being forced to recognize that the finite can only exist within the infinite without necessarily taking a course in quantum physics. Hello? Are you still with me? *It means we not only need to accept the infinite as the causal point of our existence, we need to loosen our tight grasp of the finite, mentally, and learn to follow our heart's guidance, trusting in the synchronicity of the infinite.*

At this point in recovery from addictions, most Human Beings are confused to distraction, mentally. Alcoholics and addicts at this time in their metamorphosis, are quite comical and endearing, at the same time. The child-like mixture of humility, frustration, bewilderment and pleasant surprise is a testament to the spiritual nature of recovery in Twelve Step Fellowships.

Steps Four & Five

Here Bill Wilson suggests it is of substantial importance to make a list of all our resentments, harms done, fears, and sexual misconduct. Through doing this and looking **squarely** (Freemasons will love this) at the motivation behind our misconduct or character defects we can gain real insight into our thought pattern programming. This is where the cleansing waters of truth have gotten muddied. We're led to realize that self-centered FEAR is the motivator behind all of our "defects of character" or "questionable survival instincts" which is brilliant and true, but the **vital importance of connecting that awareness with our misunderstanding of God, and who and what we are, is completely missed,** thereby providing the Risen Son Bunch ample room to hijack the awakening from within, once again. **It's crucial at this point to understand how our belief in the infinite, if connected with a "God of Fear" will _always_ result in manifesting those same character defects _or worse_ through seeing ourselves as _subjects_ with a herd mentality or a hive mind**.

Let me spell this out in no uncertain terms for those who can't understand Sponge-Bob Square-Pants without a secret decoder ring and a Geiger counter. If you believe that your "God" requires his only begotten son to be ritually tortured and sacrificed in order for you to escape a deserved eternal damnation, you consciously or unconsciously believe in a "God of Fear." You can then be manipulated beneath the level of conscious awareness, **because you're not conscious**, by the unconscious need for social status, financial security, and sex, not to mention food, water, clothing, shelter etc. Remember the definition of Humility: "The clear recognition of who, and what, we..." Spiritual Consciousness – infinite and eternal – with a unique physical manifestation having to do with our Birthday - "are, followed by the sincere desire to become what we could be." This awareness is given a catastrophic twist when we consciously believe that we're born sinners and will naturally make infinite errors in judgement, without even trying, that will require our eternal torment without the suffering and ritual blood sacrifice of a "Pure" and "sinless" "God" to spiritually take us off the hook. By believing in this Illuminati spiritual manipulation we've enslaved ourselves and our children for millennia. Through breaking the chains of addiction and remembering what and who we really are, and being true to ourselves, Mankind is waking up and the Illuminati are highly motivated to put the icing on their cake in short order.

Alexander As Helios

Apollo With Helios Halo   **Colossus Of Rhodes**

The Rising Son Bunch

To understand how intelligent, good-hearted, people can be manipulated into unconsciously subverting their innate spiritual awareness voluntarily for the benefit of those who would enslave them, one has to consciously grasp the fact that what we perceive with our five senses are the result, not the cause, of what we hold as truth in that part of our subconsciousness eternally connected with the infinite. In other words we've been conned into putting the cart before the horse through our beliefs. The cart is the finite - what we can see, hear, smell, taste, and feel. The horse is the infinite and eternal. The horse is God in other words.

I know, I just got used to thinking he was a duck, too.

By being conned into separating the cart from the horse, the physical from the spiritual, and putting the cart first, we've been manipulated into thinking we're just the cart. Not only that, we're a bad cart.... that deserves to be taken to the dump and incinerated............forever. Lucky for us, the horse is fond of us and has found a way to save us from the dump. It will require a life of sacrifice and suffering, but when we're finally taken to the dump we will magically be rejoined with the horse forever and everything will be wonderful.

Greek Sun God Helius, In His Chariot Of Fire

The Horse And The Cart

We are the horse and the cart. The cart does not exist without the horse. The horse comes first and last. The Alpha and Omega come to mind. The Alpha and Omega concept is spiritual awareness. That's what we are. That is our essence. The beginning and the end **(the cart)** that has no beginning and no end (**the horse**). Since the Bible was written in Greek by Son worshippers, it explains how the modern originators of this concept were aware of the cart and the horse analogy and purposely separated the cart from the horse and left us thinking we were simply the cart in need of the horse. The Greek word for "Sun" is "Helios." The Greek word for "Son" is "Huios." In Greek mythology the sun was per**son**ified as "Helios" and traveled around in a chariot of fire. Of course the Rising Son Bunch predate Greek mythology. Look at a picture of the mythological Greek Sun god, Helios/Helius riding around in his chariot of fire and try telling yourself that the Alpha and Omega Greeks weren't hip to the cart and the horse analogy and that putting the cart before the horse doesn't come from that awareness. We, as individuals, have been manifesting the awareness of our spiritual hijacking since before recorded history began. The Rising Son Brigade just finds a way to annex the awakening or obliterate it up until now. If you're familiar with Astrology you may be aware that because of the energy of Pluto and Uranus affecting us at this time, many of the things that were hidden are now being exposed and the Rising Sun Bunch is powerless to hide from those who are authentically looking for and following the truth where it leads. Thank God there are a few of us who don't have 401k's invested in waking up Mars with our snoring. The cart is a vehicle through which the horse experiences itself subjectively. The cart in the larger sense is the physical universe.

The Law Of Attraction & Being True To Yourself

Are you still looking for a savior and trying to get people to follow you? If so, you're a tool for the Rising Son Bunch. One of the most well known tools of the Rising Son Bunch was a slick character by the name of Billy Graham.

Whenever a high profile Illuminati puppet we refer to as President of The United States gets into ethical problems in the collective conscience or consensus trance, this slick cat is dragged out on TV and into the front pages of newspapers and magazines to offer absolution. Our language is programmed with this Illuminati symbolism. "Absolute" is a word that means total or complete. Few people recognize its esoteric origins. "Ab" is short for Abba, meaning "Father" in Hebrew. "Sol" stands for "Sun/Son", and "Ute" stands for the divine Feminine as in "Uterus." This refers to the Pagan trinity, all the way back to Nimrod, Tamuz, and Semiramis. This is not just a coincidence. Like the lead detectives in much television programming are fond of saying, "I don't believe in coincidence." Billy Graham is the most popular Baptist Evangelist in the world. If I had followed my birth vision according to the consensus trance, I would have become a Baptist Evangelist. More specifically, I would have become a Conservative Baptist Missionary, the reason being because my Father was a Conservative Baptist Missionary. I love my Father. I respect my Father. He's a good man. He's a brave man. He's an intelligent and funny man.

He learned to speak French, Swahili, and Malagasy fluently after he was grown, married and started raising a family. I always wanted to be like my father. Until Bob Dylan, John Lennon, and Paul Simon came along, that's what I was going to be, a Conservative Baptist Missionary. Dylan, Lennon, and Simon reminded me of my authentic birth vision. They absolutely ruined Billy Graham for me. We were in Hawaii in the mid sixties after the Rising Son Bunch took out JFK, blamed it on Oswald, and planted LBJ in his place. Slick Billy came out to Hawaii Crusading. My Dad took his entire congregation to see him. It was an impressive spectacle. No one suspected him of being a shill for the Rising Son Bunch. Billy can hypnotize with his polished good looks, his distinctive accent, and his voice.

Everybody just assumes God has blessed him I guess, sort of like David Rockefeller. No one stops to think, where a backwoods boy like Billy comes up with the financing and marketing ability to rent out and fill up huge stadiums with divergent denominations, sects, and beliefs year after year. Is it just the Vatican who realizes how much money there is in marketing Jesus? I don't think so. Not that my Dad was on the take, he wasn't. He was more like Smedley Butler...drank the kool-aid at an early age. Like Warren Zevon said in his song, "Looking For The Next Best Thing", "Took Sinbad seven voyages to see that it was all a ruse." My Dad's still on cruise number 6. I jumped ship in the early seventies, came back to get married and jumped again in the early nineties.

Anyway, Billy Graham uses a hymn for his "Come to Jesus" altar calls, which reminds me of chip time at A. A. meetings. The hymn is very emotional and has the benefit of what seems like about 50,000 people all singing and crying in unison. It's a Marine recruiter's wet dream. 50,000 people all sobbing in unison after anguishing their way through "The Old Rugged Cross" with George Beverly Shea. If the Marines could just set up a table at the foot of the podium and co-opt the Salvation Army's name for an hour or two at every **Crusade**, we'd have a Global Battalion we could send against Venus in three years time, tops. Poor girl!

Anyway, the hymn is "Just as I am." "Just as I am without one plea, but that thy blood was shed for me.....Oh Lamb of God, I come, I come."

 I know, I just got used to thinking of God as a horse, too. Anthropomorphism is a big word you'll come to incorporate into your vocabulary if you make it past the third degree in Freemasonry or if you have a birth vision that includes following the truth where it leads. Billy Graham uses the hymn "Just as I am" which takes the words the Christian Bible says God used to identify himself to the Pharaoh in the Old Testament; "I am", and gets 50,000 people to sob in unison their unconscious awareness of what they are, and their voluntary consent to subjugate who they are to this scapegoat or "Lamb of God" who none of them have ever seen or even know that he is what Billy Says he is, or for that matter, that Billy is what he says he is. In his book "Codex Magica" Texe Marrs, who is himself an evangelical Christian, reveals Billy Graham to be a tool of Freemasonry, which is definitely not Christian.

Here's a shot of the Reverend Schuler and Gorbechov advertising that they're Masonic Brothers. What most people fail to realize is that Christianity itself is a tool for the Rising Son Bunch, who are Satanic. Satanism is real and it's what's running the world presently because most of Humanity is in denial of what and whom they are. This is about to change. I want to do my part like David Icke and John Lennon. I'm not blind to the fact that the Rising Son Bunch has been using all of us. Whoop de doo! As we wake up out of our denial it's part of the Rising Sun methodology to divide and conquer. Alex Jones, who has done much to raise Human awareness, once accused David Icke of polluting the Conspiracy Field with his awareness of Reptilians. Ken Adachi, who has an incredible web site, full of outside the box information, directly conflicts with David Icke's astute (*in my opinion*) observations on monatomic gold. Michael Tsarion takes offense at Freeman's uncanny ability to convey much of the same information he's been chronicling. It's important to remember the Law of Attraction and the Law of Allowing. Using the Gnostic meaning of the word, for ***Christ's sake* don't throw the baby out with the bath water.**

The Importance of Teaching Spiritual Awareness

If we were taught Spiritual Awareness from our youth, we'd be able to see right through the supreme, theologically based, manipulative, divisiveness of religions and private International Central Banking Cartels. If we were taught Spiritual Awareness from our youth, it would be obvious to us all that wars and governments were manipulated by and for the benefit of those behind the religions and private central banks. Elitism and Hierarchy are tools through which our innate Spirituality is corrupted. Another man who has done so much to expose these things was **Aaron Russo**.

He became aware of the false nature of what we've been fed as truth in the United States and made some incredible movies about it. When he ran for

Governor of Nevada, he was approached by Nicholas Rockefeller, who was trying to recruit him for the Council On Foreign Relations. Aaron was flattered at first and a friendship developed. Over the course of time Aaron began to realize that the elitist agenda he was being solicited to join, while on the surface might seem like a good move for him and his family, was in direct conflict with his soul. In fact, the analogy of selling his soul to become part of the elite was quite appropriate. This all happened before 9/11. Nick told him there would come an event that would trigger war in Afghanistan so they could control the vast petroleum resources in the Caspian Basin and Iraq and build strategic bases for further conquest in the region. Nick laughed and said that from this event we'd send our troops looking in caves for the mastermind and how this would be a war without end because when you declare "War on Terror" how would anyone ever know when they've won? He said eventually they were going to microchip everyone after a catastrophic economic collapse and that only the chipped would be able to buy and sell. For the elite, a position in which he was offering to Aaron, there would be a special KMA designation on their chip. If they were ever pulled over by a cop, he would tell the cop reading his chip through his decoder to "Kiss My Ass." The so-called elite, who are cynical in the extreme, talk like this among themselves all the time. So when we hear terms like "Diplomatic Immunity" in the "Land of the Free" and the "Home of the Brave", understand that "Diplomatic Immunity" has always been an encrypted term for elite puppets meaning "Kiss My Ass." The Monarchy was not overthrown in America in 1776, the year of the official founding of the Bavarian Illuminati, It just went underground using encrypted terms like Democracy, Republic, Election, Freemasonry, and "Separation of Church and State." Aaron Russo is a great example of what we all are being guided spiritually, very strongly, to do. When tempted like the Gnostic Christ, to put the cart before the horse, to see ourselves as separate from others, and do something we know is wrong for our own benefit or immediate gratification at the expense of others in the physical world, he turned it down. Aaron, who was Jewish, did not fall for the offer from Rockefeller, who is Zionist. Aaron, whose eyes were opened by all of this, especially after 9/11, and the resulting mindless wars it was used to create, went on to make the incredible documentary, "From Freedom To Fascism" exposing the Federal Reserve Bank and the unconstitutional I. R. S. that keeps Americans enslaved. Video interviews of him exposing all of this can be found on the "Conscious Media" web site as well as Alex Jones' Prison Planet. The Illuminati have an incredible array of unconventional, high tech weaponry at their disposal and it's very likely he was targeted. He died shortly after the release of that documentary.

Dan Aykroyd as Job

Aaron Russo's Spiritual discernment in the cinema was not limited to documentaries about the Private International Banking Cartel known as the Federal Reserve, which are an Illuminati cash cow and a vampire on the people of the United States. He helped produce the movie "Trading Places" with Dan Aykroyd and Eddie Murphy. To me it's a modern day expose of the story of Job and the God of the Old Testament. In "Trading Places", Dan Aykroyd plays the part of Job. Two elderly stockbrokers known as the Duke Brothers play God and the Devil. Don Ameche plays the part of God Almighty,

Don Ameche as God almighty

wagering that his man, Winthorpe, (Job) is genetically superior through breeding, which is the cause of his good fortune with the stock market. Ralph Bellamy plays the part of the Devil and spices up the Biblical version by saying not only could he make a criminal out of Winthorpe, (Job) he could make a successful stock broker out of Billy Ray (Eddie Murphy), a street hustler. They bet one dollar. In the movie version of Job, God (Don Ameche) loses the bet, but it doesn't end there.

Ralph Bellamy as The Devil

The genius of the movie is the subtle way it exposes Biblical mythology for the rank intellectual masturbation that it is. We're responsible for our beliefs and if we choose to see God as a ruthless, old, male, gambler with the forces of darkness, using Humanity as Guinea pigs simply because we can't recall where we were when leviathan was created, we only have ourselves to blame when our God is exposed as something infinitely less than true.

That seems to be what the ones who fed us this tripe now have in mind. They're in the process of exposing Christianity while simultaneously counting on most of us being incapable of perceiving why. This is because of the procession of the Equinoxes. Oh that's right, Christians aren't supposed to study astrology, the awareness of which comes from the same source as Christianity. Pity. If they had, they'd know we were passing out of the Age of Pisces and into the Age of Aquarius and therefore we'd need a brand new Rising Son to take Jesus' place in the New Age because people in the New Age will be aware that a savior is just a scape goat for people to siphon energy off of people who don't know who and what they are. Of course for Christians this will fit in nicely with the Anti-Christ and End Times programming. The Rising Son Bunch took the Gnostic Christ and the Astrological Cross and turned them into symbols for psychic vampirism. The Gnostic Christ is another name for your heart. Listen to and follow your heart. The Gnostic Christ is the third and final principle in the Gnostic Holy Trinity and it corresponds with your heart, as the Divine Feminine corresponds with the right hemisphere of your brain, and the Divine Masculine corresponds with the left hemisphere of your brain, in which most of humanity (Men and Women) find themselves stuck. Of course the people who invented genuflecting wouldn't know anything about the Pineal gland, its relationship with Humpty Dumpty, and how fluoride will crystallize it and make it show up like the mark of the beast on an MRI. Please don't pretend that you think that I'm saying that your ego or mine is the God of the Universe.

The Celtic Cross, which Christianity loves to identify itself with, is an ancient astrological symbol of the point within the circle or the Sun within the Earth's annual rotation. This 360-degree circle is bisected vertically at the equinoxes, and horizontally at the solstices. It divides the 12 signs of the Zodiac into four equal segments of three which is graphically encrypted in Leonardo Da

Vinci's "The Last Supper" which Jordan Maxwell has revealed and Dan Brown has trotted out for the smoke and mirrors effects.

The Christian Jesus and The Cross are used to get Humanity to stay in collective denial of our own personal responsibility to be true to ourselves and not recognize what we're creating through pretending to be ignorant of our own divinity. It's like making a mistake and blaming it on the guy standing next to you; exactly what intentionally happened on 9/11. Oh, it wasn't 19 Muslim Fundamentalists with box cutters who hated us for our freedom? Forgive me, Jesus. I'm just a poor sinner whose taxes are paying for: Shock & Awe, Moab, Guantanamo, Abu Ghraib, Fallujah, Extraordinary Rendition, White Phosphorous, & Depleted Uranium. Oh, you mean it probably wasn't 19 Muslim Fundamentalists with box cutters in the first place? There really are people who enjoy war as long as you're the ones doing the killing and dying? They wear suits and ties and we worship them? It's the Rising Son Bunch who intend to use Christianity, The Federal Reserve Bank, The I. R. S., and 9/11 to bring America down from the inside? By feigning ignorance of our own authentic responsibility to recognize what a massive Red Herring 9/11 was, and the abominable evil it was used to perpetrate on the people of Iraq, Afghanistan, Gaza, and ultimately; the World, the Rising Son Bunch intend to use their manipulated control of the awakening to bring their New World Order into absolute power with World War Three, bio, chemical, nuclear, and directed energy wave weapons, the micro-chip, and our fear. My purpose in writing this book is to help my brothers and sisters in this dimension who are waking up spiritually to discern the connections between addictions, money, religions, politics, war, hierarchy, fear, and the Rising Son Bunch, and as we learn to be true to ourselves and follow our hearts, we won't throw the baby out with the bath water.

Pictures

Page 5, Double Alaskan Rainbow, Where Rainbow Rises - Wikipedia.com

Page 6, Sistine Chapel - Wikipedia.com, smiley face - Wikipedia.com

Page 7, Trojan Horse - Wikepedia.com

Page 8, Santa Claus - Wikipedia.com

Page 9, Musical Chairs - Wikipedia.com

Page 10, Bohemian Grove Sacrifice – David Dees Illustrations

Page 12, Alcoholics Anonymous - Wikipedia.com

Page 14, USMC Major General Smedley D. Butler – Wikipedia.com

Page 15, War Is A Racket - http://www.lexrex.com/enlightened/articles/warisarackethtml

Page 16, 17, Top Contractors 2007 - http://www.govexec.com/features/0807-15/0807-15s2s1.htm

Page 18, Obama's Inauguration - David Deesillustration.com

Page 19, Rupert Murdoch - Wikipedia.com

Page 21, Humpty Dumpty - Wikipedia.com

Page 22, An Inconvenient Arrest – David Deesillustrations.com

Page 25, Yin Yang – Wikipedia.com

Page 26, Indigo Point within the Circle - www.expansions.com

Page 27, Gaza, River of Blood – David Deesillustrations.com

Page 29, & 30, God Bless The Child/Billie Holiday/Arthur Herzog Jr. - Lyricsfreak.com

Page 31, Iceberg - Wikipedia.com

Page 32, Baron Guy De Rothschild, - Wikipedia.com

      Queen Elizabeth II - Wikipedia.com

      John D. Rockefeller - Wikipedia.com

Page 33, Bill O'Reilly - Wikipedia.com

Page 34, Plaque at entrance to Disneyland/Walt Disney - Wikipedia.com

Page 34, Donald Duck - Wikipedia.com

      Walt Disney - Wikipedia.com

      Walt & Werner Von Braun/Walt Disney - Wikipedia.com

Page 37, Bob Dylan - Wikipedia.com

Page 39, David Icke - David Deesillustration.com

Page 41, 666 The Number Of The Beast - The Freeman Perspective

Page 42, 666 The Number Of The Beast - The Freeman Perspective

Page 44, Osiris - Wikipedia.com

Page 45, Vatican City - Wikipedia.com

Page 46, General Electric - Wikipedia.com

      NBC - Wikipedia.com

Page 47, Dick Cheney - Wikipedia.com

Page 48, Las Vegas - Wikipedia.com

      National Cathedral - Wikipedia.com

Page 49, Washington D.C., Las Vegas, Days Inn Logo - Wikipedia.com

Page 50, Obama Campaign symbol, Chicago Sun Times - Wikipedia.com

Page 52, Dave Van Ronk - Wikipedia.com

Page 54, Akhenaten, Nefertiti, & children – Wikipedia.com

Page 55, Baron Guy De Rothschild, Rockefeller – Wikipedia.com

Page 56, Queen Elizabeth II & Prince Philip – Wikipedia.com

Page 56, Bushes, Clinton, Pay Respects To Pope – Wikipedia.com

Page 57, Gerald Ford – Wikipedia.com

Page 58, Jesus Christ - Wikipedia.com

Page 59, Jesus Christ - Wikipedia.com

Page 60, Japanese Flag - Wikipedia.com

Page 61, Tibetan Flag - Wikipedia.com

Page 62, Israeli Flag - Wikipedia.com

Page 63, Nazi Flag, Maltese Cross - Wikipedia.com

Page 64, 65 The United States Presidents Since the Assassination of JFK -   Wikipedia.com

Page 66, Barackhenaton & Apophis – FreemanPerspective.com

Page 67, Prince William - Wikipedia.com

Page 68, NATO Flag, U.N. Symbols – Wikipedia.com

Page 69, Federal Reserve Bank, Wikipedia.com

Page 70, CIA, Mossad, MI5, MI6 – Wikipedia.com

Page 71, Sunrise – Wikipedia.com

Page 72, New Orleans – Wikipedia.com

Page 74, Albert Einstein - Wikipedia.com

Page 75, 76, Donald Rumsfeld - Wikipedia.com

Page 77, Colonel Philip J. Corso - Wikipedia.com

Page 80, George H. W. Bush - Wikipedia.com

Page 81, William Jefferson Clinton - Wikipedia.com

Page 82, Fasci & the Dollar Bill - Wikipedia.com

Page 84, Double-headed eagle, 9/11 - Wikipedia.com

Page 85, Oklahoma City Bombing, 9/11 - Wikipedia.com

Page 86, War on Terror - Wikipedia.com

    Shock & Awe - Wikipedia.com

    Abu Ghraib - Wikipedia.com

    Iraq Oil Fields – businessinsider.com

    Caspian Basin – Wikipedia.com

Page 87, Osama-Tim Osman –
http.homelessonthehighdesert.wordpress.com

Page 89, Box-cutters, – Wikipedia.com

Page 90, NORAD – Wikipedia.com

Page 90, Richard Meyers – Wikipedia.com

Page 91, FAA, Baphomet, GW Statue – Wikipedia.com

Page 93, John Lennon - Wikipedia.com

Page 95, Tom Brokaw, Hunter S. Thompson - Wikipedia.

Page 96, Bill Wilson – AA History In Photos

Page 97, Rowland Hazard – AA History In Photos

Page 97, Carl Jung – Wikipedia.com

Page 100, Carl Jung – Wikipedia.com

Page 102, Double-headed eagle - Wikipedia.com

Page 103, Dayton Ohio Members, 1942 - AA History In Photos

Page 105, FDR - Wikipedia.com

Page 107, Indigo point within the circle – www.expansions.com

Page 107, Jesus Christ - Wikipedia.com

Page 109, John D. Rockefeller - AA History In Photos

Page 111, David Rockefeller - http://www.bilderberg.org/rockef.htm

Page 112, Georgia Guide Stones – Wikipedia.com

Page 113, Motorola, Washington D.C. - Wikipedia.com

Page 114, Columbia, Star of David, Freemasonic Compass & Square - Wikipedia.com

Page 115, Stairway In Israeli Supreme Court – vigilantcitzen.com

Page 116, Prometheus - Wikipedia.com

Page 119, Confession - Wikipedia.com

Page 121, 122, Helios - Wikipedia.com

Page 123, Helius - www.theoi.com/Titan/Helios.html

Page 123, A, Omega – Wikipedia.com

Page 125, Billy Graham - Wikipedia.com

Page 126, Billy Graham - Wikipedia.com

Page 127, Marine Corps - Wikipedia.com

Page 128, Lamb of God – Wikipedia.com

Page 129, Codex Magica, Rev. Schuler & Gorbechov - http://texemarrs.com/

Page 130, Aaron Russo - Wikipedia.com

Page 133, Don Ameche, Ralph Bellamy - Wikipedia.com

Page 134, Trading Places - Wikipedia.com

Page 135, Celtic Cross - Wikipedia.com

Page 136, Da Vinci's "The Last Supper" - Wikipedia.com

About The Author

Bob Prester is a 55 year old pastel colored, African American Shaman with polka dots. He was born in 1955, in Ruanguba, Congo to Pastel colored Conservative Baptist Missionaries. It didn't take Bob long to figure out that his mission, should he choose to accept it, was to study hard and return to Congo one day to save Africa for Jesus.

Bob knew he had the perfect set up for his life except for one little question that no one could answer but himself that he kept tripping over: "How important is the truth, anyway?"

So Bob dropped out of the Conservative Baptist Missionary College and set off across America alternately looking for, and hiding from the answer to that question. He made a lot of friends and worked at a lot of different jobs before a death forced him to take a peek at the answer.

Bob, whose heroes were John Lennon, Paul Simon, and Bob Dylan, decided to join the Marine Corps. The Marines taught Bob the importance of discipline and that he was an alcoholic and a drug addict and kicked him out. Bob began to realize that he needed a female companion or even with his newfound awareness of discipline, alcoholism & drug addiction he was going to lose the will to live.

Bob met Sylvia. Bob was very happy. He began looking at the answer to his question on Wednesdays and Fridays and occasionally on Saturdays. Soon Bob began to realize the Truth wasn't just the Most Important Thing, it was the Only Thing. He decided to write a book about it. He really hopes you like it and tell all your friends.

www.ingramcontent.com/pod-product-compliance
Lightning Source LLC
Chambersburg PA
CBHW041532220426
43662CB00002B/37